pq- D0125645
pq- DII - 768

LAS VEGAS

THEN & NOW

Thunder Bay Press
An imprint of the Baker & Taylor Publishing Group
10350 Barnes Canyon Road, San Diego, CA 92121
www.thunderbaybooks.com

Produced by Salamander Books,
an imprint of Anova Books Ltd.
10 Southcombe Street, London W14 0RA, UK

"Then and Now" is a registered trademark of Anova Books Ltd.

© 2013 Salamander Books

All notations of errors or omissions should be addressed to Thunder Bay Press, Editorial Department, at the above address. All other correspondence (author inquiries, permissions) concerning the content of this book should be addressed to Salamander Books, 10 Southcombe Street, London W14 0RA, UK.

ISBN-13: 978-1-60710-750-7
ISBN-10: 1-60710-750-3

The Library of Congress has cataloged the original Thunder Bay edition as follows:

Chung, Su Kim.
  Las Vegas, then & now / Su Kim Chung.
    p. cm.
  ISBN-10: 1-60710-582-9
  ISBN-13: 978-1-60710-582-4 (hardcover)
1. Las Vegas (Nev.)--Pictorial works. 2. Las Vegas (Nev.)--History--Pictorial works. I. Title.
F849.L35C485 2012
979.3'13500222--dc23
        2012019172

Acknowledgments
To Mom and Dad for their continual patience with my unending writing projects and for watching my giant fur baby George; to Larry Gragg for patiently and thoroughly reading drafts and offering brilliant suggestions; to Peter Michel and Patricia Iannuzzi for their ongoing support during the writing process; and for my work colleagues David Schwartz, Joyce Moore, Delores Brownlee, and Kelli Luchs—many thanks for all of your support and assistance with facts and photos. To historians Michael Green and Dennis McBride, two gentlemen that I am proud to call my friends, thanks for your advice and speedy responses! And to cultural heritage gurus Brian Alvarez, Mark Hall-Patton, and Courney Mooney, thank you for coming through in a pinch with images and facts. Many thanks to others who have also helped with this and/or the first edition, including Kathy War, Frank Wright, Guy Rocha, Liz Warren, Nanyu Tomiyasu, Eugene Moehring, George Stamos, Stephanie Molina, and Riva Churchill. And lastly, to Frank H. and Karl M. for putting up with my continual changes and occasional fussiness!

Picture Credits
The publisher wishes to thank the Special Collections Department, University of Nevada, Las Vegas, for kindly providing all the "then" photographs for this book. Additional credits and other sources are as follows:
Courtesy of the University of Nevada, Las Vegas Library: pages 6 (Elbert Edwards Collection); 8, 10, 11, 16 (Helen J. Stewart Collection); 12 (Garside Collection); 17 (Doris Hancock Collection); 18, 20, 74, 124 (Union Pacific Railroad Collection); 20, 22, 28, 48, 50, 52 (Ferron Collection); 24, 56, 34, 72, 76, 80, 86, 90 (Manis Collection); 26, 130 (Elton and Madelaine Garrett Collection); 19, 54 (Sunnie Gillette Collection); 30 (Maureen and Fred Wilson Collection); 32, 33 (E. W. Cragin Collection); 14, 42, 70, 100, 102, 130, 126 (Las Vegas News Bureau Collection); 64 (Frontier Hotel Collection); 132, 133 (Sands Hotel Collection); 94 (Marshall L. Wright Collection); 96 (Dunes Hotel Collection); 92, 112, 128 (Single Item Accession Collection); 67 (Howard Hughes Collection); 110 (M. Toutounji Collection); 114 (Aladdin Hotel Collection); 134 (Rockwell Collection); 138 (Wm. S. Park Collection); 142 (Bureau of Reclamation Collection).
Corbis Images: pages 84, 98, 113, 116, 119.
Getty Images: pages 23, 36, 37, 47, 68, 69, 79, 83, 97, 106, 109, 111, 120, 125, 142.
Library of Congress: pages 8, 13, 142.
Postcard Collectors Inc: pages 15, 25, 41, 43, 45, 47, 61, 65, 73, 79, 87, 89, 93, 98, 101, 106, 113, 115, 121, 123, 135.
UNLV Photographic Services: pages 41, 44, 45, 46, 53, 55, 58, 60, 62, 66, 78, 104, 118, 122, 131, 134, 140.
The photograph on page 136 was kindly supplied courtesy of the Tomiyasu family.

All "now" photography © Anova Image Library/Karl Mondon, with the exception of the photographs on the following pages:
Anova Image Library/Simon Clay: pages 75, 127.
Anova Image Library/Barrett Adams: page 67.
Anova Image Library/David Watts: pages 9, 11, 17, 19, 25, 51, 65, 73, 77, 81, 85, 89, 91, 97, 125, 127.
Bureau of Reclamation (photo: Andrew Pernick): page 143.
Las Vegas News Bureau: page 45
Wes Isbutt, Studio West, courtesy of Park Place Entertainment: page 130.

All photographs of the Venetian Hotel appear courtesy of the Venetian Resort-Hotel-Casino.

Printed in China

1 2 3 4 5 17 16 15 14 13

LAS VEGAS

THEN & NOW

SU KIM CHUNG

THUNDER BAY
P·R·E·S·S

San Diego, California

In just over a hundred years, Las Vegas has transformed
from a desert railroad outpost into the gambling and
entertainment capital of the world. The phenomenal
population growth of the past several years added another
dimension to the transformation. And the ascendancy of
Las Vegas as a model of a postindustrial metropolis has
inspired a torrent of scholarly inquiry and social
commentary from sociologists, historians, and journalists
intent on uncovering the "real" Las Vegas.

The existence of Las Vegas hinges on one simple thing:
water. The city's harsh desert surroundings would be
unlivable if not for the natural springs that have flowed
underground for centuries, creating an oasis in what is now
the Las Vegas Valley. Unfortunately, no photographic
evidence exists of what the area looked like when Spanish
explorers and traders stopped at the springs in the early
nineteenth century and named the site Las Vegas—"the
meadows"—after the lush grass that fed on the springs.
Still photographs taken in the early twentieth century
provide an idea of how the springs may have looked when
explorer John C. Frémont and other travelers rested there
while trekking through the unforgiving Mojave Desert
during the previous century.

Before long, the valley became host to a more permanent
settlement. In 1855, Mormon colonists from nearby Utah
set up a mission not far from the springs. The harsh living
conditions and an unsuccessful mining venture led them
to abandon the mission in 1858. But within a few years,
the land they had farmed was incorporated into a ranch
belonging to Octavius Decatur Gass. The property was sold
to Archibald Stewart in 1882, and after Stewart's murder,
his wife, Helen, successfully ran the ranch until 1902,
when it was sold to the San Pedro, Los Angeles and Salt
Lake Railroad. Photographs taken around this time show
remnants of the original fort as it looked on the ranch
property, and illustrate the stark, dramatic landscape of
early Las Vegas. The driving force behind the railroad,
Montana senator William Clark, carved up the property to

LAS VEGAS
THEN & NOW INTRODUCTION

create Clark's Las Vegas Townsite, which was auctioned off on May 15, 1905, a date that marks the city's birth.

Contemporary photographs of the Mission-style railroad depot, ice plant, and railroad cottages illustrate how the city's existence revolved around the railroad. Other early photographs capture the frontier quality of Fremont Street, the city's main business thoroughfare, and Block 16, the city's infamous red-light district. The isolation of desert life in early Las Vegas, with its dirt streets and tumbleweeds, is also apparent in these photographs. Images of Las Vegas in the 1920s and 1930s show a desert town that is slowly evolving into a city. The streets have been paved and are lined with graceful shade trees, and permanent public buildings such as schools and courthouses have been erected, along with luxurious private residences. The construction of Boulder Dam (now Hoover Dam) at a site just thirty miles south of Las Vegas proved to be a significant boost to the city's economy. During the dam's construction, which spanned from 1931 to 1935, thousands of workers and their families flocked to the area, and photographs reveal how the town promoted itself as the "Gateway to Boulder Dam" to attract tourists. The legalization of gambling in 1931 attracted even more tourists, who were eager to fill the gambling halls and hotels that sprang up along Fremont Street, or who wanted to take advantage of Nevada's liberal marriage and divorce laws.

As the raw western gambling halls evolved into refined casinos, neon became a popular element of signage. Photographs from the 1940s capture the most dramatic development in the history of Las Vegas—the construction of the first resort-style casino/hotels along Highway 91, the future Las Vegas Strip. Before 1941, this largely deserted four-mile stretch of road was home to a few small gambling clubs, but everything changed with the opening of the El Rancho Vegas that year. The combination of a casino within a luxury resort hotel was far removed from anything that existed on Fremont Street, and El Rancho Vegas's success soon inspired others to build similar establishments along Highway 91. Although Benjamin "Bugsy" Siegel's Flamingo generally gets the most press, it was actually one of four resort hotels constructed on the Strip in the 1940s.

The 1950s saw the continued construction of Strip resorts, each one more spectacular than the last. Contemporary photographs illustrate the diverse styles of hotels such as the Desert Inn, Sahara, Sands, Riviera, and Dunes as they changed the flat desert landscape forever. The new resorts relied on entertainment even more than gambling to attract tourists in a competitive market, and the 1950s also witnessed the introduction of showgirls as featured attractions in production shows such as Lido and Folies Bergère. City officials and hotel owners were eager to market Las Vegas as a resort and convention destination in the 1950s, even promoting the atomic blasts at the nearby Nevada Test Site as a tourist attraction. The Strip's landscape changed again with the addition of Caesars Palace—a precursor to the themed megaresorts that would characterize Las Vegas hotel development in the future.

Images of the Strip from the mid-1970s reflect dramatic changes in the Las Vegas landscape as existing resorts replaced their bungalow-style hotels with high-rises, and the Strip's skyline slowly grew upward.

Photographs of Las Vegas today reveal a downtown that is almost unrecognizable from the city's early days as a railroad outpost. The Strip is packed with luxury megaresorts, the result of a hotel-building boom that revitalized the city in the 1990s. These photographs also capture the disappearance of the public structures that helped to define the city's history, and hotels that were a reflection of its mystique and excitement. Although Las Vegas is no different from many American cities in this respect, the high-profile destruction of these structures in public implosions has given the city a reputation of having little respect for its past. Others, however, see this as just an unavoidable byproduct of a city that is constantly reinventing itself. Ultimately, with its glamour, its neon, its brash excess, and, yes, its tackiness, Las Vegas has captured the world's imagination. To those who are familiar with the city only through popular stereotypes, these photographs may serve as an education and a revelation. To those who live in Las Vegas, they may bring back nostalgia and a pride of place that the city much deserves.

Railroad Depot, 1910   p. 12

Union Pacific Station, 1942   p. 14

Fremont and Main Looking East, 1950   p. 23

Northeast Corner of Main and Fremont, c. 1930   p. 26

Second and Fremont Looking West, 1950   p. 36

El Cortez Hotel, 1946   p. 42

Helldorado Parade, 1963   p. 44

Las Vegas Post Office, c. 1949   p. 56

Flamingo Hotel, 1955   p. 72

Sands Hotel, 1953   p. 82

Stardust Hotel, 1960   p. 88

Dunes Hotel, 1955   p. 96

Caesars Palace, 1966   p. 100

Aladdin, 1976   p. 114

Boardwalk Casino, 1998   p. 116

Landmark Hotel, 1970   p. 122

McCarran Field, 1952   p. 134

Hoover Dam, 1931   p. 142

LAS VEGAS SPRINGS
A rare oasis in the Mojave Desert

LEFT: Some 10,000 years ago, underground springs erupted through the desert floor and created an oasis of lush, grassy meadows in the Las Vegas Valley. Known only to local Indian tribes for centuries, it wasn't until the nineteenth century that Spanish and American explorers made this natural water supply known via travel diaries and maps. In fact, it was Spanish explorers who named Las Vegas—"the meadows"—after the lush grass that grew around the abundant springs. In May 1844, explorer Captain John C. Frémont wrote of his stop at the springs on one of his many government-sponsored expeditions to the western United States. Working with the U.S. Army's Topographical Corps, Frémont was the first to list Las Vegas on an official government map. Although his report described the taste of the water at the springs as good, but "rather too warm to be agreeable," Frémont did find that they afforded a "delightful bathing place," as witnessed many years later.

1906

BELOW: Evidence of rudimentary irrigation canals, seen here channeling Las Vegas's precious resource.

1907

ABOVE: The 180-acre Las Vegas Springs Preserve opened in 2007, and is composed of the Origen Museum, historical walking trails, an outdoor amphitheater, botanical gardens, and the Desert Living Center.

BELOW: By 1950, southern Nevada's 41,000 residents demanded more groundwater than nature could supply. A decade later, the population had almost tripled, worsening the problem. Despite having also tapped into nearby Lake Mead, the Las Vegas Springs had dried up by 1962. In the 1970s, the once life-giving springs were almost paved over, but Dr. Claude Warren of the University of Nevada, Las Vegas, conducted an archaeological survey that helped reroute the new expressway (I-95) around the site. In 1978, concerned citizens and the Las Vegas Valley Water District successfully petitioned to add the springs to the National Register of Historic Places. This eventually led to the creation of the Las Vegas Springs Preserve: a center for regional culture, wildlife, and history on the site. In October 2011, the Nevada State Museum and Historical Society opened on the grounds of the preserve. In addition to a research library and archives that provide access to important documents and photographs on the region's history, the Nevada State Museum provides an opportunity for tourists and locals alike to learn about the history of Nevada and Las Vegas.

c.1900

LAS VEGAS FORT
Mormon missionaries established an early settlement in Las Vegas

ABOVE: The availability of an abundant water supply in this otherwise harsh desert valley prompted Mormon missionaries from Salt Lake City to organize a Las Vegas settlement in 1855. At a site just four miles east of the Las Vegas Springs, the missionaries farmed crops and constructed an adobe fort for protection that was later abandoned in 1858. Sections of the original fort, along with a ranch house added by Helen Stewart, are visible in this photo from circa 1900.

THE FIRST LADY OF VEGAS
The fort site and thousands of surrounding acres were purchased by miner and rancher Octavius Decatur Gass in the 1860s. When it was ruled that the property was actually part of the Nevada territory, he found he owed a large amount of back taxes and his financial problems made him lose the property to Archibald Stewart. In 1881 Stewart moved his family, including his wife Helen and their four children, to the ranch in the middle of the desert. Just a few years later, in 1884, Stewart was murdered in a dispute at the neighboring Kiel Ranch. In true pioneer fashion, however, Helen remained at the ranch and, with the aid of farmhands and her children, managed to make it thrive until she sold it to the San Pedro, Los Angeles, and Salt Lake Railroad in 1902. As one of the pioneers of the early desert town, she was nicknamed the "First Lady of Las Vegas."

ABOVE: The fort later became part of the Las Vegas Rancho property that was sold to the San Pedro, Los Angeles, and Salt Lake Railroad (SPLASL) in 1902. The property and the fort were then leased for various purposes over the years, until the fort's decay caused concerned citizens to have it named to the National Register of Historic Places in 1972. After a lengthy restoration, the property opened as the Old Las Vegas Mormon Fort State Historic Park in January 2000. The site of the oldest surviving structure in Nevada, the facility is maintained by the organization Friends of the Fort. In September 2008, the Friends of the Fort and other community groups worked together to erect a statue of Helen Stewart on the fort grounds in honor of her role as the "First Lady of Las Vegas." On December 3, 2011, sculptor Benjamin Victor's life-size statue of Helen Stewart was officially dedicated in a ceremony at the Las Vegas Fort in the presence of city officials, community organizations, and Stewart's descendants.

1910

RAILROAD DEPOT / PLAZA HOTEL
The railroad depot was instrumental in driving the development of Las Vegas

1910

LEFT: In 1902 Senator William Clark purchased the Las Vegas Rancho property on behalf of the San Pedro, Los Angeles, and Salt Lake Railroad. On May 15, 1905, the land, now carved up into parcels, was auctioned off as Clark's Las Vegas town site. This view looking southwest from the top of the Arizona Club in 1910 shows how quickly the town took shape. The prominent mission-style building is the railroad depot, constructed near Fremont and Main in December 1905. A contemporary newspaper article from the *Las Vegas Age* described the outer walls of the depot as buff-colored with contrasting terra-cotta tile roofing. The two-story building had telegraph rooms and dressing rooms for the train crews on the second floor, while most of the first floor was taken up with a large waiting room, ticket office, baggage room, and "a ladies waiting room of liberal proportions."

RIGHT: Almost a hundred years later, there are few reminders of the important role the railroad played in the development of downtown Las Vegas. Where once the residents were dwarfed by the vastness of the surrounding desert, today tourists are dwarfed by the hotel high-rises and canopy of the Fremont Street Experience. The recently renovated Plaza Hotel stands tall on the site of the original railroad depot with its modernistic dome. The hotel itself was constructed on the park grounds of the former railroad depot, and the actual tracks still remain behind the hotel.

ABOVE: This panoramic view shows the park that was later added to the front of the depot, which stood far back from Main Street. In March 1908, several hundred trees were donated by leading Las Vegas citizens as a way to beautify the park.

13

1942

UNION PACIFIC STATION / PLAZA HOTEL
The station was demolished in 1970 to make way for the Union Plaza Hotel

New Union Pacific Station, Las Vegas, Nevada

Gateway to Boulder Dam

ABOVE: The *City of Las Vegas* was the passenger train operating between Las Vegas and Los Angeles in December 1956. In September 1961, the train was renamed the *Las Vegas Holiday Special*. The service was discontinued in June 1968.

LEFT: In 1940, the gleaming new Union Pacific railroad station took the place of the original mission-style Salt Lake Depot at Main and Fremont. Contemporary publicity described it as being in the "typical modernistic western motif" style and billed the Union Pacific Station as "the first streamlined, completely air-conditioned railroad passenger station anywhere." Over the years, the station became something of a downtown landmark. In the 1950s and 1960s, a typical Saturday night for Las Vegas teenagers would include "dragging" Fremont Street in their cars, and then driving around the circle in front of the Union Pacific Station.

ABOVE: After passenger train service to Las Vegas was discontinued, the twenty-six-story Union Plaza Hotel was constructed just in front of the original Union Pacific Station as a joint venture between the Union Pacific Railroad and a private corporation. The hotel opened on July 2, 1971, with what was then the world's largest casino. Downtown casino mogul Jackie Gaughan, one of the original partners in the Plaza's construction, became its main owner in 1993, and renamed the hotel Jackie Gaughan's Plaza Hotel and Casino. In March 2004, Gaughan sold most of his downtown properties, including the Plaza. It was closed briefly in 2010 in order to carry out a number of renovations to the aging property. The $35 million renovation included extensive changes to the lobby, casino, guest rooms, and suites, bringing a sleek new look to the Plaza's decor with elegant furnishings, fixtures, and coverings purchased from the Strip's Fontainebleau Resort after it suspended construction. The renovated hotel opened in August 2011 and later that year, Oscar Goodman, the popular and gregarious former mayor of Las Vegas, opened Beef, Booze & Broads, an upscale steakhouse, in the elevated dome space in front of the hotel.

1906

ARIZONA CLUB / BINION'S PARKING LOT

It started life as a bar, but soon added a brothel

ABOVE: The beautiful leaded glass windows of the Arizona Club made it one of the most elegant buildings on Block 16.

TOP RIGHT: Shortly after the Las Vegas town site was established, all liquor sales were restricted to an area on First Street between Ogden and Stewart known as Block 16. Peppered with saloons and brothels, the area soon gained a reputation as the town's red-light district. One of Block 16's most famous bars was the Arizona Club, shown here as it looked in 1905 when it was a simple wood-and-canvas tent with a false front. At its grand opening in March 1906, the new Arizona Club showed itself to be a far cry from the crude shack it had been just months before. The mission-style club was constructed out of concrete blocks, which were considered a stylish building material at the time. In addition to its leaded glass windows and solid oak doors, the interior featured an elegant, hand-carved, thirty-foot-long mahogany bar. The building was lit primarily by gaslight, with electricity reserved for special occasions. In addition to beer and whiskey, patrons could try games such as nickel slots, faro, roulette, and blackjack. Although the Arizona Club had initially been a respectable establishment, its new owner, Al James, added a second story in 1907 that featured rooms and prostitutes and placed the bar firmly within the Block 16 tradition.

RIGHT: On December 1, 1941, the commanding officer of the nearby Army Air Corps Gunnery School threatened to declare Las Vegas off-limits to his men if the city didn't do something about its red-light district. The following day, local police raided the Block 16 brothels and saloons, and many, including the Arizona Club, were later shut down. Today the Binion's Horseshoe parking lot and garage rests on this infamous site. Brothel prostitution did not actually vanish from Las Vegas at the closing of Block 16, though; after the war, it moved to other areas of town.

1910

FIRST AND FREMONT FROM OGDEN

A view looking toward the all-important Las Vegas Ice Plant

ABOVE: Another view of downtown, looking south on First Street toward its intersection with Fremont Street in 1910, shows the pioneer character of the town. The signage marking the Thomas Department Store on the southwest corner is barely visible; it was part of the building known as the Opera House, which provided space for entertainment and meetings until it burned down in May 1912. Undaunted by losses of approximately $58,000, owner M. C. Thomas was determined to rebuild his store, which supplied Las Vegas residents with groceries, domestic goods, and clothing. Although faced with a number of obstacles, Thomas and his partner Proctor Smith finally reopened the store in September 1914. No doubt the female residents of the tiny desert town were grateful, as the Thomas Department Store was one of the few places in early Las Vegas that sold the latest fashions.

ICE PLANT AT MAIN AND BONNEVILLE
Before the days of refrigerated railroad cars, the ice plant was the most important building in Las Vegas. The original Armour Ice Plant had burned down in July 1907, leaving the town without this precious commodity until the new plant (shown above) was completed in April 1908. The Pacific Fruit Express Company constructed the new 100-ton plant. It was also responsible for supplying ice to the Las Vegas community and generating electricity for the railroad and the town. After its railroad contract ended, the ice plant continued to produce ice on a commercial basis. By 1983 the building sat vacant and was eventually declared unsafe and demolished in May 1988. In 2003, the Ice House Lounge opened near the ice plant's original location and was decorated with historic photographs of old Las Vegas. It closed in 2009.

ABOVE: A proliferation of hotel towers and parking garages has dramatically changed the look of downtown Las Vegas, obscuring the view of the surrounding area. The latticed-steel "celestial vault" covering some four blocks of Fremont Street is part of the Fremont Street Experience. In addition to serving as a venue for nightly light shows, the canopy provides shade for pedestrians during the day. Just visible in the right center of the image is the California Hotel, part of the locally owned Boyd Gaming empire. The California Hotel, or "the Cal" as it is known by its guests, has long catered to visitors from the Hawaiian Islands. Boyd Gaming patriarch Sam Boyd grew to love the informal and friendly atmosphere of the islands during the five years he spent in Hawaii in the 1930s, and he sought to re-create it at the California Hotel and Casino. Today almost 70 percent of the hotel's guests come from Hawaii.

FIRST AND FREMONT LOOKING WEST

The location of Vegas's iconic cowboy, now silent and motionless

BELOW: A banner proclaiming "Key Pittman for U.S. Senator" can be seen stretched across Fremont Street in this 1916 photo. Horse wagons mingle with early automobiles on unpaved streets in a view looking west toward the railroad depot from Fremont and First. At right is a similar view, taken some thirty years later, and shows the glut of neon signs that had begun to transform Fremont Street into "Glitter Gulch." The Pioneer Club has taken the place of the Thomas Department Store at the southwest corner of First and Fremont, but its full-length neon cowboy Vegas Vic would not be added to the property until 1951. The Vegas Vic icon was actually created a few years earlier in the 1940s by the noted J. Walter Thompson Advertising Agency on behalf of the Las Vegas Chamber of Commerce. It was used for a number of years in many Las Vegas advertising campaigns and on their stationery and collateral before it was transformed into three-dimensional form. Designed by the neon sign pioneers YESCO, Vegas Vic weighed approximately six tons and cost Pioneer Club owner Tudor Scherer $28,000. It took the company three days to install him atop his perch.

1916

1946

BELOW: The friendly neon cowboy Vegas Vic keeps a watchful eye on the hundreds of tourists who stroll down Fremont Street each day. Originally, the famous fifty-foot-tall cowboy waved his mechanical arm, boomed a friendly "Howdy, partner" to passersby, and generated smoke rings from his cigarette. Today the Glitter Gulch icon still greets tourists and locals alike, but he was silenced during the shooting of a Lee Marvin movie in 1966. A quarter-century later, his arm gave out. Now quiet, motionless, and a few feet shorter (to make room for the Fremont Street Experience canopy), Vegas Vic remains a symbol of old-time Las Vegas friendliness and hospitality. During a 1998 restoration, his shirt was painted in the red-and-yellow checked pattern that is seen here.

c. 1930

FREMONT AND MAIN LOOKING EAST
A street that has witnessed the evolution from gaslight to neon light to LED

1950

LEFT: Looking east on Fremont from the tree-lined park in front of the railroad depot around 1930, the banner proudly declares the city as "The Gateway to Boulder Dam." It was an auspicious time for Las Vegas. In 1931, the quiet little railroad town, which had struggled financially in the 1920s after its railroad repair shops were moved to Caliente, Nevada, was about to get a boost from two significant events. That year the Six Companies began construction on Boulder (later Hoover) Dam, bringing employment to thousands of men. Legalized gambling also came to Nevada in March 1931, and with it crowds of tourists who left their money behind in casinos and hotels and provided a boost to the Las Vegas economy. Twenty years later (above) the park is still there behind the camera, minus a few trees, but the skyline over Fremont is crammed with distinctive neon signage. As the main business thoroughfare of Las Vegas in the 1950s, the street was host to both casinos and hotels, as well as stores such as J.C. Penney and the family-owned Ronzone's Department Store.

ABOVE: In this contemporary view looking east on Fremont Street from the Plaza Hotel, the railroad station and its tranquil park are long gone and the ninety-foot-high Fremont Street canopy is a prominent sight. Once bustling with traffic, it is now part of the Fremont Street Experience, a pedestrian mall that stretches from Main to Fifth Street. A collaboration between the City of Las Vegas and downtown casino owners, the Fremont Street Experience project was part of a $70 million effort to revitalize downtown Las Vegas in the mid-1990s. In the evening, a spectacular computer-generated light show sweeps across the concave underbelly of the 1,400-foot-long structure. During each six-minute show, a state-of-the-art, 540,000-watt, concert-quality sound system pumps through more than 200 speakers. In June 2004, a $17 million upgrade by LG Electronics helped boost the attraction's visual technological capabilities to include over 12.5 million synchronized LED modules. Like the Las Vegas sign and Vegas Vic, the Fremont Street Experience has become an instantly recognized symbol of the city.

NEVADA HOTEL / GOLDEN GATE

Recipient of Las Vegas's first telephone in 1907

BELOW: The Hotel Nevada was built in January 1906 and was described in early advertisements as a "substantial concrete building." A year later, the first telephone in Las Vegas was installed at the hotel in the office of Charles "Pop" Squires, a true local pioneer who arrived in 1905 and played many important roles in early Las Vegas, but was probably best remembered as editor of the *Las Vegas Age* newspaper. One of the paper's regular columns was a list of the Hotel Nevada's arrivals and provides a fascinating insight into visitors both local and national who came to Las Vegas in its early years. The hotel was later enlarged and renamed the Sal Sagev (Las Vegas spelled backward) in 1931. The Sal Sagev was the scene of many raucous Helldorado celebrations in the 1930s, and its bartender Sid Martin was famous for his sloe gin fizz.

c. 1911

RIGHT: The Golden Gate Hotel is shown in 2002 (above) and after the opening of the Golden Nugget's new tower in 2009 changed the skyline behind it dramatically (below).

RIGHT AND BELOW RIGHT: In 1955, the Golden Gate began operating as a casino underneath the Sal Sagev Hotel. By 1974, it had become successful enough to assume the entire operation, and the property was renamed the Golden Gate Hotel. Today, this historic property still features many original wood fixtures from its earlier incarnations and has long been the smallest hotel on Fremont Street. The building underwent a major restoration in 1990, bringing back some of the building's original historical luster. The Golden Gate's shrimp cocktail has been a longtime Las Vegas tradition, and in 1991, the hotel had a large party to celebrate serving 25 million shrimp cocktails. In 2011, work began on a new expansion to the hotel, the first in fifty years, which will see a new lobby and five-story tower added to the Golden Gate. The tower will add some 30,000 square feet and is slated to bring a fresh look to the Golden Gate's facade.

c.1930

NORTHEAST CORNER OF MAIN AND FREMONT

Legalization of gambling turned the New Overland Hotel into the Las Vegas Club

ABOVE: The "new" Overland Hotel as it appeared circa 1930. The original hotel, built in 1906, burned down in 1911. A large wraparound balcony distinguished the hotel's appearance. The curious signage proclaiming "Big Free Sample Room" referred to a room where salesmen could display their wares (not a free hotel room) and was a precursor to those provided to modern convention vendors. A phone directory from 1926 listed E. A. Beckett as proprietor, and advertised rooms with hot and cold water "with or without bath" at room rates of $1 to $3.

ABOVE: The Overland Hotel became the Las Vegas Club in 1931 when legalized gambling returned to Nevada. For many years it featured the tallest neon sign (120 feet) on Fremont Street. Its current facade reflects the hotel's sports-themed casino design. The Las Vegas Club's Sports Hall of Fame reportedly features the most complete collection of baseball ... to all the sports mementos, the casino is known for dealing "the most liberal twenty-one in the world," based on its lenient, player-oriented blackjack rules on splitting, doubling down, and winning on any six-card total under twenty-one. In November 2010, its casino began operating the only bingo room in downtown Las Vegas.

1917

WHARTON DRUG Co.

NORTHWEST CORNER OF FIRST AND FREMONT
The Las Vegas Pharmacy and Hospital was a big step up from a tent with ten cots

ABOVE: The Las Vegas Pharmacy, shown here around 1917, occupied the first floor of this castlelike structure on the northwest corner of First and Fremont. From about 1906 to 1920, the upper story served as a small hospital and was run by Dr. Roy Martin, one of the first physicians to set up a practice in town. Four months after his arrival in August 1905, Martin was named chief surgeon for the Las Vegas and Tonopah Railroad. The heat and primitive conditions were challenging in these early days, and Martin's railroad practice consisted of a tent with ten cots and a makeshift operating room. Martin and his fellow

FIRST STATE BANK

Just opposite the Las Vegas Pharmacy, on the northeast corner, was the First State Bank (pictured left), the second bank to open in Las Vegas. Shown here as it looked shortly after its completion in January 1906, the bank was solidly constructed out of concrete blocks. The building featured a classical facade with a colonnaded portico, and an interior that included marble floors and mahogany wood fixtures. The bank proved instrumental in funding the development of much of early Las Vegas, including both homes and businesses.

doctor Halle Hewetson usually sent patients to Los Angeles for serious operations, but any surgical procedures they did perform were done at 4:00 a.m. during the coolest part of the night. It was quite an upgrade for Martin when he moved his hospital to the suite of offices on the second floor of this First and Fremont location in June 1906—in addition to a dozen beds, it housed a pharmacy. Martin was also instrumental in creating a larger hospital on the corner of Second and Fremont in 1917, and contracting architect A. L. Warwick to build the Las Vegas Hospital at the corner of Eighth and Stewart in 1931.

ABOVE: The Las Vegas Pharmacy closed around 1955 and was then remodeled and replaced by a succession of small casinos. It operated as Sassy Sally's for many years until the late 1990s, when it was replaced by the Jules Verne–themed Mermaids Casino. In addition to offering that most southern of delicacies, the deep-fried Twinkie, Mermaids Casino is famous for the colorfully attired ladies who stand in front of its entrance and ply passersby with offers of shiny strings of Mardi Gras beads. The historic First State Bank was demolished in 1958 to make way for the Bird Cage Club, which was later absorbed by the Mint Casino. A 1965 expansion added the twenty-six-story tower and spectacular pink neon facade that made the Mint one of downtown's most colorful casinos. In 1988, the Mint and its tower were purchased by and absorbed into its next-door neighbor, Binion's Horseshoe. TLC Casino Enterprises purchased the property in March 2008, but the economic downturn that has affected much of Las Vegas led its new owners to close the tower and thereby suspend the hotel side of their operations in 2009.

1925

WEST FROM FIFTH AND FREMONT

Showing the important role played by shade trees in early Las Vegas

ABOVE: The residential character of Fremont Street is apparent in this view taken near the intersection of Fifth and Fremont in 1925. Some twenty years after the founding of Las Vegas, one of the most distinctive features of this portion of Fremont Street is the proliferation of shade trees. Tree planting served both a cosmetic and practical purpose in early Las Vegas. The trees not only created a more civilized look in the flat and dusty desert surroundings, but also provided much-needed shade from the treacherous heat of the Las Vegas summer in the days before air-conditioning. Eucalyptus and cottonwood trees (as seen in this photo) were two popular varieties planted in early Las Vegas. In fact, one of the earliest civic beautification projects taken on by the ladies of the Mesquite Club after its founding in 1911 was planting trees along Fremont Street.

ABOVE: Fifth Street, now an extension of Las Vegas Boulevard, marks the eastern boundary of the five-block Fremont Street Experience. The houses and shade trees disappeared long ago, and in their place is the Neonopolis complex to the right. At its May 2002 opening, city officials hoped that the open-air shopping, food, and entertainment complex decorated with antique neon signs would aid in the revitalization of downtown Las Vegas. Sadly, that was not the case, and challenges—namely a lack of foot traffic and sustainable businesses—have plagued Neonopolis since its opening. In the ten years since, tenants have come and gone, and only a few remain today, among them Telemundo Studios and the aptly named hamburger joint Heart Attack Grill. Hennessey's Tavern is located across the street in the world's largest "pint glass."

1934

EL PORTAL THEATRE /
INDIAN ARTS AND CRAFTS

The cinema is gone, but the historic neon
sign remains

ABOVE: The El Portal Theatre at 310 Fremont opened on
June 21, 1928, with a prescreening of Clara Bow's film *Ladies
of the Mob*. With its organ loft and orchestra pit, the theater also
served as a venue for plays, music recitals, and vaudeville
shows. It was one of the first buildings in Las Vegas to install
air-conditioning—a feature its owners were eager to promote, as
this photo from the mid-1930s demonstrates. The interior of the
El Portal was decorated in a Spanish motif and featured a lobby
bordered in colored tiles. Hand-painted ceiling beams and
chandeliers completed the elegant interior, which had a seating
capacity of 713 including eighty-four cushioned high-back loge
chairs. Further down the street at 202 (right) was the Fremont
Theatre. Built in 1947 and owned by Lloyd Katz for many years,
the theatre was the site of numerous movie premieres, including
the world premiere of *The Las Vegas Story* in 1952. The film
starred Jane Russell, Victor Mature, and Vincent Price.

1954

1934

ABOVE: By the late 1950s, the tiny El Portal struggled to compete with the larger theater venues in Las Vegas. After the theater closed in the late 1970s, the building became home to El Portal Gifts. Today it houses the Indian Arts and Crafts store. Traces of its glory days remain in the original neon sign that decorates the front, and in the heavy wood ceiling beams that decorate the store's interior.

LEFT TOP: The Fremont Theatre as it appeared in 1954 with the classic Rock Hudson and Jane Wyman film *Magnificent Obsession* on the marquee.

LEFT BOTTOM: The interior of the El Portal was decorated in a Spanish motif with hand-painted ceiling beams and chandeliers. It had a seating capacity of 713 and included eighty-four cushioned high-back loge chairs.

c.1943

FREMONT STREET
LOOKING EAST

Las Vegas boomed in the 1940s, and nowhere
was this more evident than on bustling
Fremont Street

ABOVE: A view of bustling Fremont Street looking east in the
1940s shows a landscape of tightly clustered casinos, businesses,
and neon signs. Although gambling establishments were
dominant, Fremont Street also served as the town's main
business district at the time, with banks, drugstores, and liquor
stores for residents and visitors. The 1940s were a time of great
transition for Las Vegas and especially Fremont Street. Tourists
poured into the town, as did new residents, many of them
soldiers (and their families) stationed at the Las Vegas Army Air
Corps Gunnery School, marines from Camp Sibert near Boulder
City, defense workers from the Basic Magnesium Plant in

nearby Henderson, and troops from the Desert Warfare Center south of Searchlight. For the gaming establishments and hotels that dominated Fremont Street, there was growing competition from the casino hotel resorts on Highway 91, such as the El Rancho Vegas and Last Frontier that had been constructed just south of the city limits in 1941 and 1942, respectively. The plush and spacious resorts offered amenities not available in the smaller downtown casinos. For the city, it was an alarming development, as the new resorts were located outside of the city limits and therefore not subject to city taxation.

ABOVE: Fremont Street looks anything but a typical American city today. No longer the town's main business thoroughfare, it is a pedestrian mall designed to entice tourists to visit downtown Las Vegas. Casinos still line the street, but souvenir shops and gift kiosks have taken the place of other businesses; the Pioneer is now strictly a gift shop. Mardi Gras beads, slot machines, and frozen margaritas are the order of the day at the Louisiana-themed La Bayou casino, while the Hawaiian chain ABC Stores provides a host of Hawaiian comestibles to ensure that the numerous visitors to "Hawaii's Ninth Island" (their nickname for Las Vegas) are never short of the comforts of home.

1950

SECOND AND FREMONT LOOKING WEST

With one of Las Vegas's classic neon signs, the Golden Nugget was impressive both day and night

ABOVE: Fremont Street in daytime took on a different atmosphere than the street at night when it lived up to its "Glitter Gulch" nickname. The spectacular open-frame neon sign atop the Golden Nugget, 48 feet high and 48 feet wide, was designed by Hermon Boernge of the Young Electric Sign Company and installed in 1948. The "gold nugget" at the top of the sign was 12 feet wide, and its neon rays spread 26 feet. Designed in an elegant Barbary Coast style, the hotel itself opened in August 1945, and was owned by Guy McAfee. A former Los Angeles police captain and gambling operator, McAfee had left California and moved to Las Vegas in 1939.

ABOVE: Over fifty years later, the Golden Nugget is still a vibrant part of Fremont Street, but was transformed into an elegant resort by Steve Wynn in the mid-1970s. In an area where neon reigns supreme, the restrained gold-and-white exterior makes its own statement. It contrasts sharply with the vibrant blue-and-gold neon of Binion's Horseshoe, which replaced the Eldorado Club in 1951. The Golden Nugget has long been regarded as the most elegant of the downtown hotels, and recent renovations by new owners Landry's Restaurants have made the hotel an even more attractive spot. One of its most popular attractions is the award-winning Tank pool and jacuzzi, which features a 200,000-gallon shark tank and a three-story waterslide. In November 2009, the completion of phase three of its renovation added a new 500-room hotel tower with an entrance accented by the dramatic vertical fish tank of the Chart House restaurant.

HOTEL APACHE

The Hotel Apache with its distinct neon sign first opened in March 1932, but it was not until 1946 that the Eldorado Club took over the first floor. Like many of the early downtown hotels, the Apache served as a gathering place for Las Vegans who took part in the festive Helldorado celebrations. Until the mid-1940s, the Hotel Apache also played an interesting role in Las Vegas policing, which was relatively unsophisticated in the city's early decades. Owing to the fact that early squad cars had no radios, the city's police would signal officers in the surrounding streets by flashing a large red light atop the hotel.

1962

NEVADA CLUB
Operators of an unusual profit-sharing plan

ABOVE: The colorful Nevada Club, located at 109 Fremont Street, originally opened as the Fortune Club in December 1952. After three years, additional room on the east side of the building was carved out, and in 1957, the former Western Union Building adjoining on the west side was purchased. In June of that year, the three sections were patched together under the seventy-five-foot Nevada Club marquee shown in this photo. In 1959, the Nevada Club's profit-sharing plan was the first of its kind in a Nevada casino and was under study for approval by the state tax commission. Publicity was achieved via the casino's monthly newsletter, *This Is Las Vegas*, which served to promote the Nevada Club and provide tourist information on other Strip and Fremont Street happenings.

ABOVE: In summer 1969, the owners of the Golden Nugget bought the adjoining Nevada Club property for $1.25 million. By 1970, the owners had purchased or obtained long-term leases for almost the entire city block on which the Golden Nugget was located, and announced tentative plans to construct a huge hotel and casino complex that would include a fifty-story tower. In 1973, a young businessman named Steve Wynn took over the Golden Nugget after acquiring a majority interest in the public company that owned it. He was elected company chairman at age thirty-one, and it was with his direction that the Golden Nugget underwent significant renovations in 1974. Wynn continued to upgrade the hotel and constructed its first tower in 1977. Diamond Jim's Nevada Club, as it was known in the 1960s, lives on today in the postcards, casino chips, and souvenir items that serve as a reminder of its brief but colorful time as one of the reigning casinos of Glitter Gulch.

1953

ATOMIC TESTING
Vegas Vic was happy to welcome the nearby atomic testing

1955

LEFT: A white mushroom cloud from the nearby Nevada Test Site overshadows Vegas Vic in this famous photo taken on April 18, 1953. Set up by the U.S. government in 1951, the Nevada Test Site was located in the barren desert just sixty-five miles northwest of Las Vegas. Between 1951 and 1955, some forty-five aboveground tests were conducted at the site and could be seen hundreds of miles away in cities and towns in Nevada, Arizona, California, and Utah. Most residents were blissfully unaware of the dangers, and the town promoted the blasts as another Las Vegas tourist attraction. Resorts offered "atomic cocktails," and tourists watched the early morning blasts from their hotel balconies. Las Vegas hotel publicity machines even managed to mix photos of showgirls (above) with atomic testing in promotions for "Miss Atomic Bomb" and "Mis-Cue."

ABOVE: Although Vegas Vic still stands watch over Fremont Street, the skyline is no longer visible, hidden under the "celestial vault" of the Fremont Street Experience. The dramatic mushroom clouds that used to be a prominent sight in Las Vegas during atomic testing days ceased to be an attraction when underground testing became the norm after 1962. Las Vegas citizens later realized that the blasts they had watched for entertainment purposes were anything but harmless. In 1978, the federal government began investigating the establishment of a permanent nuclear waste repository at Yucca Mountain, a site just eighty miles northwest of Las Vegas, near the original Nevada Test Site (now the Nevada National Security Site). Most southern Nevadans have been adamantly opposed to the project, and the fate of Yucca Mountain has become one of the most controversial questions in modern Nevada.

1946

EL CORTEZ HOTEL

A fifty-nine-room hotel was a major development
in the downtown Las Vegas of 1941

ABOVE: Marion Hicks and J. C. Grayson built the El Cortez,
downtown's first major resort, for $245,000 in 1941. Like many
buildings of this era, the fifty-nine-room hotel was designed in
the mission style with a Spanish tile roof. Critics felt the hotel's
location at Sixth and Fremont was too far from downtown to
make a profit, but it was apparently profitable enough to attract
the attention of East Coast mob figures looking to buy a casino.
For a brief period in 1945, the El Cortez counted among its
owners Benjamin "Bugsy" Siegel, Meyer Lansky, Gus
Greenbaum, Moe Sedway, Davie Berman, and Willie Alderman.
In 1963, Jackie Gaughan purchased the El Cortez from J. Kell
Houssels and immediately set about expanding the hotel.

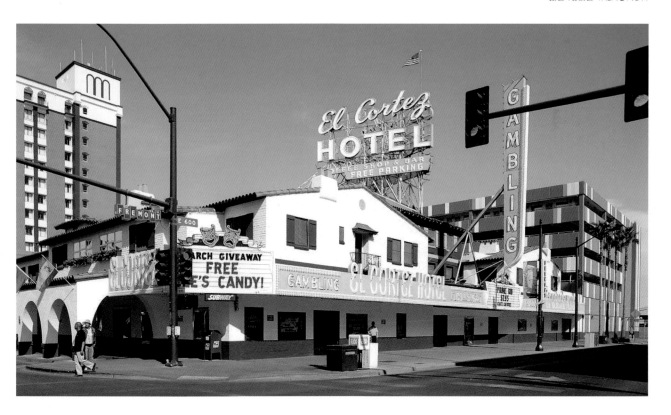

ABOVE: One of the few downtown buildings to retain its original facade, the El Cortez looks much the same as it did over sixty years ago. Aside from the satellite dishes on the roof and a few bars on the windows, the addition of an adjacent high-rise is the biggest change to the hotel's exterior. Locals declared it the "end of an era" when longtime owner and casino pioneer Jackie Gaughan sold his stake in the El Cortez in May 2008. Although Gaughan's business partner and friend Kenneth Epstein and his family now run the hotel, Gaughan was still resident in a suite upstairs in 2012, and his spirit of friendliness and personal service remains an important part of the El Cortez's appeal to locals. The hotel has undergone extensive renovations in recent years, including the transformation of the overflow Ogden House property into the boutique-style Cabana Suites. The El Cortez is also considered one of the anchor properties of the recently renovated Fremont East District, which runs from Las Vegas Boulevard to Eighth Street and includes pedestrian walkways, landscaping, new bars and restaurants, and colorful new neon signage.

HELLDORADO PARADE

The parade started off as a celebration of the city's Western heritage

ABOVE: Helldorado remained a popular Las Vegas community celebration for many decades. In the 1940s and 1950s, attendance at the parade was a given for Las Vegas residents, and participation in the parade was a regular part of any Strip hotel's promotional efforts. Sadly, as the population of Las Vegas grew larger, it became more challenging to continue the various Helldorado traditions, and by 1997, the celebration was put on hold for financial reasons. In 2005, as Las Vegas celebrated its centennial, the Elks felt it was time for Helldorado to make a comeback. With the pedestrianization of Fremont Street, the parade route has changed, and it now runs in the early evening.

LEFT AND ABOVE: Las Vegas's Helldorado celebrations began in April 1934 with a parade organized by the local Elks Club as a way of exploiting the (then) small town's Western heritage. Eagerly embraced by residents and city leaders who saw the tourists the parade could bring to a city in the midst of a depression, it quickly became an annual event. A few years later the Elks added a rodeo to the celebration. Initially located in a park next to the downtown business area, the four-day event had grown large enough by 1942 to be moved to the newly constructed Cashman Field on north Fifth Street. Just adjacent to the field, volunteers constructed a Helldorado Village with hitching posts, watering troughs, and other Western artifacts. A number of colorful traditions also played a part in the early Helldorado celebrations. Although all participants dressed in Western garb, the town's male citizens would grow beards for a competition that judged them on length and style. Still another humorous tradition was the Kangaroo Court in which participants were arrested and thrown into a faux jail set up on Fremont Street. Yet nothing captured the spirit of a Helldorado celebration more than the parades. By the early 1950s, there were three parades, and it was the Sunday beauty parade that typically featured floats entered by the Strip hotels and downtown casinos, as exemplified by the Space Age Sands Hotel float shown above.

49°

The MINT   The MINT

The MINT

Hotel Fremont

CASINO

FREMONT

1968

THE MINT

The setting for Hunter S. Thompson's infamous
Fear and Loathing in Las Vegas

LEFT: A spectacular wave of bright pink neon characterized the Mint Hotel, which first opened in 1957—and was expanded in 1959—at the corner of First and Fremont. The hotel underwent its most dramatic change in June 1965 with the opening of a twenty-six-story tower that was the tallest building in Nevada at the time. The newly expanded hotel included nine restaurants, seven cocktail lounges, a Sky Deck swimming pool, and the fabulous Space-A-Vator, a glass-enclosed outside elevator that spirited patrons on a scenic ride from the street up to the Top of the Mint, where they could enjoy cocktails, dining, and dancing. Perhaps an even more entertaining activity in these early years was the hotel's "Behind the Scenes Tour," which offered visitors a chance to visit casino areas that were previously off-limits, such as the coin and currency counting room, and the "Eye in Sky" security area. Never content to rest on its laurels, the hotel sponsored additional promotional attractions, such as the famous Mint 400, an off-road desert race for motorcycles and four-wheeled vehicles that had its first run in 1969. The race gained further notoriety in 1971 when it was profiled by "gonzo" journalist Hunter S. Thompson during his infamous weekend trip to the city, chronicled in the book *Fear and Loathing in Las Vegas*. The Mint also appeared in the 1971 James Bond movie *Diamonds Are Forever*.

RIGHT: The Mint Hotel tower and its spectacular neon facade remained a colorful part of Fremont Street until June 1988, when it was purchased by the Binion family, operators of the neighboring Binion's Horseshoe. The purchase doubled the size of the Horseshoe's casino and added the twenty-six-story high-rise with 296 guest rooms to their property. Not surprisingly, they later removed the Mint's hot pink neon facade and extended the blue-and-gold neon signage of Binion's across the entire length of the property. The hotel changed hands several times in the twenty-first century.

ABOVE: The unique pink wave design of the Mint Hotel's sign was one of the most distinctive neon creations to grace Fremont Street.

c.1910

MAIN AND BONNEVILLE LOOKING EAST

The railroad cottages are an essential part of Las Vegas history

ABOVE: Looking east from Main and Bonneville around 1910, tidy rows of railroad cottages are clustered on either side of Bonneville from Second to Fourth Street. The town ends at Fifth Street, surrounded only by desert and mountains, and the isolation of living in early Las Vegas is dramatically apparent. In May 1910, the *Las Vegas Age* encouraged its citizenry to make sure that they were counted for that year's census. City officials were aware that the town had been depopulated. Five years after the auction of Clark's town site, the population of Las Vegas stood at just 800. From 1909 to 1911, the San Pedro, Los Angeles, and Salt Lake Railroad constructed sixty-four cottages to house workers and their families from the company's machine shops and railyards. Each employee cottage cost approximately $1,700 to build, and the railroad charged families rent of $20 a month for a four-bedroom house. The cottages, such as those shown here at the corner of Third and Garces (right), were constructed out of concrete blocks and wooden frames. There were three styles of homes available depending on the number of bedrooms the family needed.

c.1910

ABOVE: Time and progress have erased the frontier character of the town, and most of the railroad cottages are long gone. The desert landscape that once surrounded the tiny town has been pushed back by development on all sides. The most dramatic changes downtown have been the large-scale disappearance of residential housing, and the addition of multiple high-rises that have altered the skyline dramatically. Prominent in the background is the Clark County Regional Justice Center, which replaced the Zick and Sharp–designed Clark County Courthouse in late 2005, as well as a number of new high-rise and mid-rise condominiums that have brought a different style of residential living back to the downtown area. The railroad cottages at Third and Garces—and indeed nearly all of the cottages—slowly disappeared over the years. In April 2002, Preserve Nevada named the historic Railroad Cottage District to its list of "Ten Most Endangered Sites," and shortly afterward, both public and private entities stepped forward to preserve four of the cottages. One cottage was transferred across town to the Clark County Museum in Henderson. The other three went to the Las Vegas Springs Preserve. A handful of cottages remain in their original locations, but their appearances have been significantly altered. Modern condos (left) occupy the site of the cottages at Third and Garces.

1908

SECOND AND CARSON

Built on land donated by the railroad, Christ Church Episcopal was the second church in Las Vegas.

ABOVE: The charming Christ Church Episcopal on the northeast corner of Second and Carson is shown here shortly after its completion in 1908. Constructed on land donated by the railroad, its founding members included Las Vegas pioneers Delphine "Mom" and Charles "Pop" Squires, who were present at the laying of the cornerstone. Although Christ Church Episcopal held its first service in August 1908, the

First Methodist Church actually predated it, having been founded on June 18, 1905, just a month after Clark's town site auction that signified the birth of Las Vegas. Services were first held at the First Methodist Church, located on the northeast corner of Third and Bridger, in December 1908. It was destroyed by fire in January 1922. Catholics in the fledgling town were no doubt relieved when a priest, Father E. V. Reynolds, arrived in southern Nevada in 1908, performing the first Catholic baptism in Las Vegas in December of that year. Reynolds initially ministered not only to Las Vegas but other areas in southern Nevada, such as Caliente, Pioche, Searchlight, and Delamar, until 1910 when he settled in Las Vegas.

ABOVE: By 1953, Christ Church officials realized that they had outgrown their downtown location. A generous property gift enabled them to construct a new church at its current location on Maryland Parkway and St. Louis, and the sale of the downtown property provided funds to purchase additional land for adequate parking at the new location. The original building was destroyed soon afterward. Today, the site houses a municipal parking garage that's just a stone's throw away from the Fremont Street Experience and the Four Queens Hotel and Casino. Three hotel high-rises (shown here left to right), the Four Queens, Golden Nugget, and the D Las Vegas (formerly Fitzgeralds) provide a backdrop that even Christ Church founding member C. P. Squires could never have imagined.

c. 1911

LAS VEGAS GRAMMAR SCHOOL / FOLEY FEDERAL BUILDING

In the days before air-conditioning, school let out by the second week of May

ABOVE: On September 11, 1911, the Las Vegas School at Fourth and Bridger opened as a combination grammar and high school. The two-story mission-style structure (like so much of early Las Vegas, built on land donated by the railroad) featured a heating plant and electric fan ventilation and was a vast improvement over the three-room wooden schoolhouse on Second and Lewis that had burned down in October 1910. In the days before air-conditioning, the intense heat of Las Vegas forced school officials to dismiss classes for the summer by the second week of May. They were able to make up this time by shortening Easter and Christmas vacations. When Las Vegas High School was constructed in 1929, the school pictured here became known as the Fifth Street Grammar School.

BELOW: Children at Las Vegas Grammar take a break from playing volleyball at recess to pose for a photographer.

c. 1925

Las Vegas Nev.

ABOVE: By 1921, overcrowding led school officials to authorize construction on two additional buildings near the Las Vegas Grammar School. The following year, a kindergarten building and a manual arts building were constructed on the Fourth and Bridger site. In 1964, the three buildings were sold to the U.S. government and demolished to make way for the present Foley Federal Building on Las Vegas Boulevard (formerly Fifth Street). In 2003 and 2004, the Foley Federal Building underwent extensive renovations that completely changed its interiors, reinforced its frame to make it more bomb-resistant, and altered its facade to make it more compatible with the Lloyd D. George U.S. Courthouse across the street. The original Foley Federal Building made a cameo as a backdrop in the 1995 movie *Casino*, in a scene that featured attorney Oscar Goodman as himself and actor Joe Pesci in the role of the Tony Spilotro–inspired mob character Nicky Santoro.

53

CLARK COUNTY COURTHOUSE

Photographed after a rare snowfall, the courthouse building was abandoned in the late 1950s

BELOW: Dedicated on December 7, 1914, the Clark County Courthouse was the work of prominent Nevada architect Frederick J. DeLongchamps. The $50,000 building was designed in the Spanish Colonial Revival style and situated in the center of the courthouse square near the southeast corner of Second and Carson. During the building's construction, soil and a piece of turf from Ireland were placed in the courthouse steps by Father Reynolds, the town's resident Catholic priest, in the

1941

hopes of preventing snakes from entering the building. Reynolds believed that Irish soil was deadly to snakes, there being no indigenous snakes in the home country. The tree-shaded lawn surrounding the courthouse made a comfortable resting place for those who attended public meetings held on the courthouse steps. Offices for various county services were located on the first floor, and the district court was convened on the second floor.

c.1930

ABOVE: There was a long tradition of volunteer firefighters in Las Vegas, going back to the early days of Clark's Las Vegas town site. In their earliest incarnation, the firefighters used a hose rolled into a coil on top of a buckboard, but in the early 1920s, they finally acquired a proper truck with ladders and hand extinguishers, such as the one shown here posed in front of the Clark County Courthouse. The volunteer firefighters served honorably until 1940, when they were replaced by a professional department.

BELOW: Glass, concrete, and steel characterize the current Clark County Courthouse, designed by local architects Walter Zick and Harris Sharp in 1958. Although the original DeLongchamps structure stood next to it briefly, that was demolished soon afterward. In the 1980s, Clark County officials remodeled Zick and Sharp's original design with a two-story concrete addition and colonnade done in the Brutalist style. This building functioned as the courthouse for Clark County until October 2005, when a much larger Regional Justice Center opened at Clark Avenue and Third Street. In December 2005, then-sheriff Bill Young proposed that the building be turned into a headquarters for the Las Vegas Metropolitan Police Department, but the old courthouse proved too small for this purpose and the headquarters was ultimately moved into another building downtown. The second Clark County Courthouse was still vacant as of 2012.

c. 1949

LAS VEGAS POST OFFICE / MOB MUSEUM
From a building that hosted mob investigations to a building that hosts mob history

LEFT: The U.S. Post Office and Court House on 301 East Stewart Avenue near Third was completed in 1933 and is shown here in the late 1940s. The neoclassical structure was constructed as part of an extensive federal government building program begun in the late 1920s by the Hoover administration. In 1942, city offices moved to the building as it became a government center for about three decades. The building achieved its greatest exposure in November 1950 when its courtroom was used as the Las Vegas base for the U.S. Senate's Kefauver hearings on organized crime. The hearings moved from city to city and were televised live for an American public who watched with fascination as organized crime figures repeatedly "took the Fifth" and declined to testify for fear of incriminating themselves. In Las Vegas, many of the casino owners called to testify had conveniently left town.

ABOVE: Entered on the National Register of Historic Places in February 1983, the United States Post Office and Court House contained offices for the U.S. Tax Court, Social Security Administration, and Postal Service until April 2002, when the City of Las Vegas took possession of the historic structure with plans to turn it into a museum or educational facility. Las Vegas mayor Oscar Goodman, along with a dedicated board of directors that included former Las Vegas FBI director Ellen Knowlton, were keen to see it transformed into the Mob Museum. With the help of local historians and the creative team that put together the International Spy Museum in Washington, D.C., the museum gradually took shape. On February 14, 2012, the National Museum of Organized Crime and Law Enforcement officially opened to the public on the eighty-third anniversary of the notorious St. Valentine's Day massacre in Chicago.

1947

EL RANCHO VEGAS / HILTON GRAND
The hotel resort that helped create a radical shift in casino development

1957

EL RANCHO VEGAS / HILTON GRAND

Having led the way in the 1940s and 1950s, the El Rancho burned down in 1960

ABOVE: Highway 91 was an empty stretch of road leading into Las Vegas when California hotelier Thomas Hull, attracted by lower land and tax costs, decided to build a hotel at its intersection with San Francisco (now Sahara) Avenue. His El Rancho Vegas, with its trademark windmill accenting a ranchlike Spanish mission design, opened on April 3, 1941, and set the tone for Western-style friendliness and hospitality. It was the first resort hotel to open on what would soon be known as the Las Vegas Strip. The El Rancho Vegas had a far different look from the typical hotel high-rises that populate the Strip today. The hotel was situated on sixty-six acres of manicured lawn that featured palm trees and carefully tended flower beds.

1948

ABOVE: The El Rancho Vegas pool was deliberately located in front of the resort to attract passing cars.

RIGHT: In 1960, the El Rancho Vegas was destroyed in a suspicious fire. Although owner Beldon Katleman announced plans to rebuild the hotel, the promised resort never materialized and the lot remained vacant for years. Howard Hughes bought the land in 1970, and the late casino owner Bob Stupak even considered developing a *Titanic*-themed property on the site, but neither project materialized. In November 2003, Las Vegas's third Hilton Grand Vacation Club opened the doors of its 540-unit, twenty-seven-story tower, and the first in what was to be a series of four on the site. A second thirty-eight-story tower was constructed in 2006. MGM Resorts International (formerly MGM Mirage) purchased the 25.8-acre parcel to the north of the Hilton towers in 2007, but the land remains vacant. The aerial views on the previous pages show a landscape that has been changed dramatically by the Sky Las Vegas condominium tower south of the Hilton (to the left of the Strip), and the unfinished Fontainebleau Resort (to the right of the Strip) across the street.

1943

LAST FRONTIER

In 1942, it was the only thing in the landscape—today it's the only thing missing

1942

LAST FRONTIER /
NEW FRONTIER

The second major resort on the Strip was
originally inspired by the Old West

ABOVE: The "early west in modern splendor" was the theme
of the Last Frontier Hotel, which opened on October 30, 1942.
The hotel was decorated with authentic pioneer furnishings. It
sported headboards that resembled oxen yoke, had wagon-
wheel lighting fixtures in the dining room, and featured the old
Arizona Club's mahogany bar. To the north of the main complex
was the Last Frontier Village, a re-creation of a frontier town
that featured a stagecoach to drive patrons around the hotel
grounds, and came with its own wedding chapel known as the
Little Church of the West. The Last Frontier was sold in 1951,
and again in 1955. Its new owners would dramatically change
the hotel to reflect their theme: "The New Frontier: Out of
This World." The Old West decor was replaced with a sleek and
ultramodern "Atomic Age" design. Its exterior featured a
seventy-foot-long entrance canopy and a 126-foot trylon
(triangular pylon) tower dotted with flashing multicolor lights.

LEFT: Its transformation into the New Frontier did not significantly alter the low-rise structure of the original hotel, as can be observed in these 1950s postcards.

RIGHT: After a series of ownership changes, the hotel was demolished to make way for a new building that opened in July 1967. Howard Hughes purchased the property soon afterward and shortened its name to the Frontier. In 1988, the hotel was sold to the Elardi family and became the site of a bitter union strike that lasted more than six years until the hotel was sold to Phil Ruffin in October 1997. It was rechristened the New Frontier in 1999. The casino's owners partnered with real estate mogul Donald Trump to build the Trump International Hotel and Tower, a gold-facade high-rise luxury hotel-condominium, at the rear of the property. In May 2007, owner Phil Ruffin sold the thirty-six-acre New Frontier property to the ELAD Property Group for $1.24 billion in one of the most expensive real estate deals in Strip history. The historic resort then closed its doors on July 16, 2007, and was imploded in November of that year. The land remains vacant.

1953

1968

LEFT: The caption on the marquee advertises a 1968 heavyweight fight between Mac Foster and Joe Hempfield, when in fact the fighter's surname was Hemphill.

LEFT: The Last Frontier Village attraction was the brainchild of the vice-president and general manager, William J. Moore. Constructed adjacent to the hotel, the collection of Western-themed buildings and artifacts added an authentic touch to the Western ambience that was the hotel's trademark. The buildings and artifacts were from the collection of Robert "Doby Doc" Caudill and were sent to Las Vegas from his warehouse in Elko. Some of the larger relics included mining trains, wagons, buggies, and old cars. An extensive collection of antique firearms also formed part of the historical display. In addition to Caudill's artifacts, Moore commissioned the construction of a wedding chapel (Little Church of the West) that would fit into the Western-themed village. In 1950, the Silver Slipper casino was added next to the Last Frontier Village.

RIGHT: Although the Last Frontier Hotel and Casino was transformed into the space age–themed New Frontier in 1955, the Last Frontier Village continued to serve as a Western-style attraction for another ten years. In 1965, the owners of the New Frontier decided to tear down the hotel and construct a brand-new 500-room Frontier Hotel. The Last Frontier Village was closed at this time, and although there were rumors that it might reopen when the new construction was complete, this never happened. "Doby Doc" Caudhill, whose many Western artifacts and props made up the Last Frontier Village, dismantled it at this time and transferred the items to his home near the Tropicana Hotel. The iconic slipper today graces the Neon Boneyard Park.

1947

LITTLE CHURCH OF THE WEST

One of the most moving churches in all of Nevada

LEFT: With its liberal marriage (and divorce) laws, Las Vegas has long been a popular wedding site for both celebrities and ordinary citizens who flock to the many chapels scattered along the Strip and downtown. None could be more charming than the Little Church of the West, the oldest existing structure on the Las Vegas Strip. In 1942, Last Frontier owner William Moore commissioned Las Vegas architects Zick and Sharp to design a chapel that would resemble an existing Western-style church in California for his Last Frontier Village attraction that was constructed and assembled next to the hotel. The chapel's exterior was constructed of dark-stained cedarwood, and its interior walls lined with the same California redwood that was used in the construction of the altar. Cozy and charming, the chapel attracted many famous couples in its early days, including 1940s pinup girl Betty Grable and trumpet player Harry James. Singer Judy Garland also married her fourth husband here in November 1965. But perhaps the most famous pair wed at the Little Church of the West was not a real couple at all. Elvis Presley and Ann-Margret played Lucky Jackson and Rusty Martin (respectively) in the 1963 movie *Viva Las Vegas*.

RIGHT: A truck gets ready to move the Little Church of the West from its original location in the Last Frontier Village, one of three moves it made before reaching its current location on southern Las Vegas Boulevard near Russell Road.

1954

ABOVE: Listed on the National Register of Historic Places, the Little Church of the West is the oldest existing structure on the Las Vegas Strip and celebrated its seventieth anniversary in 2012. The chapel was moved from its original location on the north side of the Last Frontier Hotel to the south side in 1954. During the construction of the Fashion Mall in 1978, it was moved again to the grounds of the Hacienda Hotel, and in 1996, it made its third and final move to southern Las Vegas Boulevard near Russell Road to accommodate the building of Mandalay Bay. The chapel's various moves have not dimmed its popularity as a wedding site, nor its legacy as a celebrity wedding spot. Two prominent couples that have tied the knot at the Little Church of the West in the last two decades are Billy Bob Thornton and Angelina Jolie, and Cindy Crawford and Richard Gere.

c.1953

FLAMINGO
The Flamingo set new standards of excellence in Las Vegas

ABOVE: The fabulous Flamingo as it looked in the early 1950s when it was bounded by desert to its left and right. Although Southern California businessman Billy Wilkerson began construction on the resort, it was Benjamin "Bugsy" Siegel, using borrowed mob funds, who completed it at a cost that may have reached over $6 million due to shortages in building materials and Siegel's extravagance. Phoenix builder Del Webb constructed the hotel at Siegel's direction in the style of an elegant Miami resort. Siegel was responsible for bringing a level of sophistication and glamour to the Flamingo that outshone the existing Western-themed properties common at the time.

ABOVE: In July 1970, Kirk Kerkorian signed an agreement with Baron Hilton to purchase both the International and the Flamingo, which in 1971 officially became the Flamingo Hilton. Its original bungalows have been replaced by a series of high-rise towers, and landscaping no longer envelops the hotel but is confined to the space between the towers. The last vestige of the old Flamingo constructed by Siegel was bulldozed in 1993. In 1994, the Hilton Grand Vacations Club (the reddish buildings to the right of the property) was the first time-share constructed on a major Strip hotel property. The following year saw the addition of the hotel's lushly landscaped wildlife habitat, which originally housed a flock of Chilean flamingos, swans, ducks, turtles, and penguins. Despite the recent departure of the penguins to the Dallas Zoo, the habitat with its koi ponds and waterfalls remains a peaceful escape from the Strip.

1955

NIGHTTIME SHOT OF THE FLAMINGO

Benjamin "Bugsy" Siegel spared no expense on the Flamingo and it cost him his life

LEFT: Siegel's triumph at the Flamingo was short-lived. On June 20, 1947, he was killed in the living room of his girlfriend Virginia Hill's Beverly Hills home. It was generally thought that the New York mob (led by Meyer Lansky), from which he took orders, had grown tired of extensive cost overruns at the Flamingo and also suspected him of skimming cash off the top. The syndicate placed Gus Greenbaum in charge of the Flamingo soon after Siegel's death, and he ran the casino with great success until his retirement in 1955. It was during Greenbaum's tenure that the spectacular eighty-foot "Champagne Tower" with glowing neon rings was installed in front of the hotel in 1953. A Las Vegas landmark for years, it was the tallest freestanding sign structure on the Strip during the 1950s and 1960s.

RIGHT: The tower was demolished in 1968 after financier Kirk Kerkorian bought the property and made extensive renovations. Kerkorian's main agenda in purchasing the hotel was as a training establishment for employees hired to work at his soon-to-be completed International Hotel and Casino on Paradise Road. He would sell both properties to the Hilton Hotel chain in 1970. The hotel with one of the most colorful pasts in Las Vegas is fittingly adorned with some of the most spectacular neon light displays on the Strip. Designed by Paul Rodriguez and installed in 1976, the neon features swirling fuchsia and orange feathers surrounded by a band of neon-illuminated flamingos.

1956

THUNDERBIRD HOTEL / TURNBERRY PLACE

The Native American–themed resort hotel liked to be first in entertainment

ABOVE: The Strip's fourth major hotel, the seventy-six-room Thunderbird, opened on Labor Day 1948 and was located slightly south and across the street from El Rancho Vegas. The resort, with its trademark neon bird, took its name from a Navajo legend of the thunderbird as "the sacred bearer of happiness unlimited." Developed by Nevada gaming pioneer Marion Hicks (of El Cortez Hotel fame) and Nevada lieutenant governor Clifford Jones, the Thunderbird was noted for the cozy and comfy atmosphere created by three fireplaces that warmed the hotel's public area. Inside, rooms such as the "Wigwam" and "Navajo" continued the Native American theme, as did the Indian portraits. Early on, entertainment director Hal Braudis was dedicated to bringing in fine entertainment and, in his dual role as advertising director, came up with the slogan

ABOVE AND RIGHT: A sign advertising the Turnberry Place luxury condominium development is shown on the site that had once held the Thunderbird, Silverbird, and El Rancho hotel properties (photographed above in 2002). A portion of this large vacant lot next to the Riviera (closer to Paradise Road than Las Vegas Boulevard) was the construction site for Turnberry Place's four luxury condo towers. The fourth tower was completed in 2006 just before the groundbreaking for the Fontainebleau Resort, shown right with the top of one of the Turnberry Place towers visible at bottom right of the picture.

"Remember, you saw it first at the Thunderbird." Among the many firsts was the Las Vegas debut of Ella Fitzgerald in 1949. Not all the firsts at the Thunderbird were good for business, however. In 1955, it became the first hotel to have its gaming license suspended following allegations that its owners had failed to report investments made by underworld figures. After a period of litigation, the Nevada Supreme Court ruled in favor of the hotel and it continued to prove popular. In another first, show producer Monte Prosser brought Broadway's successful *Flower Drum Song* to the Thunderbird stage in 1961 in a slightly altered version that was more appropriate for Las Vegas audiences. Its success led the Thunderbird and other Strip hotels to bring in additional (shortened) Broadway shows—a tradition that continues to this day.

ABOVE: After purchasing the Thunderbird in 1977, Major Arteburn Riddle, owner of the Dunes Hotel, reopened the hotel as the Silverbird. In 1982, new owners gave it a southwestern facade and renamed it the El Rancho (not to be confused with the Strip's original El Rancho Vegas). After its closure in 1992, the new El Rancho lay vacant until Turnberry Associates, developers of the upscale Turnberry Place condominium project, purchased the site in May 2000 with plans to develop a $700 million luxury high-rise community and casino. The El Rancho buildings were imploded in October 2000 and replaced by the four forty-story Turnberry Place towers, the last of which was completed in 2006. In early 2007, construction began on the $2.9 billion Fontainebleau Resort Las Vegas on property just to the west of the Turnberry Place towers. The resort was styled after the glamorous Fontainebleau Hotel in Miami. Construction continued until the severe economic downturn led the property's creditors to halt financing for the project, forcing its owners to file for bankruptcy in mid-2009.

1951

DESERT INN / WYNN LAS VEGAS

Guests admired the nightly "dancing waters" at one of the Strip's original hotels.

ABOVE: Moe Dalitz provided the financing and Wilbur Clark served as the affable public face for the Desert Inn, which opened on April 24, 1950. The hotel's trademark colors of Bermuda pink and bright green reflected its southwestern theme and complimented a unique roof composed of white tile chips. Hotel patrons no doubt appreciated the convenience of having a thermostat available in every room, but were likely more impressed by the "Dancing Waters" that appeared nightly, accompanied by graceful music, just adjacent to the Desert Inn pool. The Desert Inn pool was one of the great attractions of the resort, so much so that it featured in promotional photographs sponsored by the Union Pacific Railroad, which were used to entice tourists to visit Las Vegas.

ABOVE: Soon after the property celebrated its fiftieth anniversary in 2000, Steve Wynn purchased the hotel for his then-wife's birthday. In 2001, Wynn announced plans to construct the megaresort Le Rêve on the former site of the Desert Inn. French for "the dream," Le Rêve was named after a Picasso masterpiece owned by Wynn and his former wife, Elaine. Implosion of portions of the old Desert Inn took place

in October 2001. The $2.7 billion luxury hotel and casino-resort opened to the public under its new name, Wynn Las Vegas, on April 28, 2005. Viewable from many Vegas vistas, the curved brown resort's finer features include 2,716 high-end guest rooms and suites, a 111,000-square-foot casino, a Ferrari and Maserati dealership, and an eighteen-hole golf course.

1955

DESERT INN / WYNN LAS VEGAS

The "hunk on the diving board" was a publicity pose copied up and down the Strip

LEFT: The Desert Inn's attractions included the Painted Desert Room, which featured world-class entertainers. In the 1960s, show producer Donn Arden brought his spectacular shows Hello America and Pzazz to the Desert Inn stage. Although Arden was famous for bringing tasteful topless showgirls to the Las Vegas Strip in the Stardust's Lido de Paris, his shows at the Desert Inn were more family-friendly. In April 1967, the Desert Inn became part of the Howard Hughes legend when the reclusive billionaire, who had taken up residence in November 1966, bought the hotel for $14 million to silence the complaints of hotel executives who wanted him to vacate his rooms for the casino's high rollers.

BELOW: Never content to rest on his laurels, Steve Wynn broke ground on the second tower of his resort on the first anniversary of the Wynn Hotel. The $2.3 billion Encore resort opened on December 22, 2008, and although its exterior was a mirror image of the Wynn, its interior look was decidedly different. Designed by Roger P. Thomas, the elegant interior was influenced by the Wynn Macau (China) property and features Asian influences with strong red colors and a whimsical butterfly motif. In this photo, the Wynn and its sister property sit side by side, two shimmering brown columns on the site of the former Desert Inn.

BELOW: The cash needed to run a casino for a single night is shown by Desert Inn employees gathered in the gambling room before the opening on May 1, 1950.

SAHARA HOTEL

The Sahara was one of the few Strip hotels to reach its golden anniversary

BELOW: The Sahara Hotel started life as the Club Bingo, a 300-seat bingo parlor at the corner of what was then San Francisco Street (Sahara) and Highway 91. In October 1952, four years after the club's opening, owner Milton Prell enlarged and remodeled the Club Bingo into the African-themed Sahara Hotel. Inside, the showroom, called the Congo Room, was flanked by statues of spear-wielding African warriors, and the Caravan Room restaurant and the Casbar Lounge continued the African theme. The famous Sahara camel statues decorated the exterior and served as a popular attraction for both tourists and locals. The fourteen-story tower shown here was added in 1966.

1966

1949

BELOW: On October 7, 2002, the Sahara celebrated its fiftieth anniversary, becoming only the fourth original Strip property (after the Frontier, Flamingo, and Desert Inn) to achieve the golden milestone. Its exterior was dramatically different, however, as a result of a number of renovations and additions over the years. The most recent renovation, completed in 1997, resulted in this Moroccan-themed structure with stylistic minarets and attractions such as the NASCAR Café and Speed roller coaster. Financial difficulties in the wake of the economic downturn that hit Las Vegas hard after 2007 proved insurmountable for the hotel, and it closed on May 15, 2011. In November 2011, the Clark County Commission approved the owner's permits to remodel the hotel, with plans to demolish the roller coaster and add a large outdoor dining area.

SANDS HOTEL / VENETIAN

Forever linked with the Rat Pack and the
Copa Girls

BELOW: The hotel most closely associated with old-time
Las Vegas glamour, the Sands opened its doors on December
15, 1952. The distinctive sign and marquee of the Sands Hotel
is shown here prior to the construction of the Sands Tower.
Designed by Hollywood architect Wayne McAllister, the hotel
featured five two-story buildings named after famous American
racetracks grouped in a semicircle around the hotel's half-moon
swimming pool. Like many Strip hotels at the time, the interior
was decorated with warm earth tones, along with murals of
Nevada scenery. Perhaps the hotel's most popular attraction was
the Copa Room, which featured the beautiful Copa Girls and a
wealth of famous entertainers, such as marquee headliners Peter
Lind-Hayes and Mary Healy, who were regulars on the Las

Vegas Strip for decades and appeared in both film and television during the 1950s and 1960s. Married for almost sixty years, the couple retired in Las Vegas. Lind-Hayes was the son of silent-screen beauty Grace Hayes, who ran a nightclub known as the Grace Hayes Lodge (formerly the Red Rooster) from 1947 to 1953 on Highway 91 near the location of the current Mirage Hotel.

BELOW: Publicity Director Al Freeman would go to any lengths to publicize the Sands during his twenty-year tenure at the hotel. Two of his most popular publicity vehicles were the endless stream of beautiful Copa Girls and celebrities who appeared at the hotel. Comedian Milton Berle was a regular at the Sands and no doubt enjoyed the attention of this bevy of beauties in this 1950s publicity shot.

BELOW: By 1996, the once-splendid Sands Hotel could no longer compete with the spectacle offered by the themed megaresorts that proliferated throughout Las Vegas in the 1990s. The hotel and its famous tower were imploded in November 1996 to make way for the Venetian resort-hotel-casino, the brainchild of billionaire casino developer Sheldon Adelson. The destruction of the hotel also provided Hollywood spectacle when footage of an airplane slamming into the soon-to-be destroyed casino was used in the film *Con Air*. Constructed at a cost of $1.5 billion, the Venetian celebrated its grand opening on May 3, 1999, amid a flurry of white doves, trumpets, and singing gondoliers. With its cobbled walkways, replica of St. Mark's Square, and reproduction of Venice's Grand Canal, its interior offers guests an Old World feel. Its exterior is one of the most beautiful and spectacular on the Strip and features replicas of Venice's Doge's Palace, Rialto Bridge, and St. Mark's Campanile. The Venetian was initially home to a branch of the Guggenheim Hermitage Museum when it opened, but the facility has since closed.

1953

Sign text: Sands — A PLACE IN THE SUN — COPA ROOM — JACK ENTRATTER PRESENTS — FRANK SINATRA — COUNT BASIE — PAT COOPER — CELEBRITY THEATRE — THE RIGHTEOUS BROTHERS — GAYLORD & HOLIDAY — BETSY DUNCAN — ERNIE STEWART TRIO — EXCITING NEW COPA GIRL REVUE — ENTRANCE — Sands

SANDS HOTEL / VENETIAN
From Rat Pack cool to Venetian elegance

LEFT: The Sands Hotel's trademark marquee is accented by the newly constructed seventeen-story Sands Tower in this 1966 photo. The tower, designed by noted architect Martin Stern, was part of a $9 million renovation completed in 1965, and was seen as a prototype for future Las Vegas high-rises. Construction of the tower displaced much of the original low-rise portion of the Sands Hotel. Stern, famous for his Googie-style coffee shops in Los Angeles, was responsible for both original designs and additions for a number of Las Vegas hotels beginning with his renovations at the Sahara in 1953. Other important designs included the Mint Hotel tower, the Flamingo mid-rise renovation in 1967, and several towers at the Riviera in the 1970s. His most important designs, however, were the International and the MGM Grand, both of which were built for businessman Kirk Kerkorian. Considered a master of resort hotel casino design, Stern brought a new style to the Las Vegas skyline with his spectacular high-rise towers. The Sands Hotel tower was imploded on November 16, 1996, to make way for the Venetian Resort-Hotel-Casino.

Sign text: FRANK SINATRA — DEAN MARTIN — SAMMY DAVIS JR. — PETER LAWFORD — JOEY BISHOP — IN THE LOUNGE

ABOVE: Constructed on the former site of the Sands Hotel, the Venetian is one of the most lavish properties on the Strip, with its 4,049 luxury suites, numerous fine dining options, luxury Grand Canal Shoppes, and a branch of the exclusive Canyon Ranch Spa. Beyond its luxurious setting, the Venetian is home to a 120,000-square-foot casino. Its entertainment is far removed from the Rat Pack and Copa Girls of yesteryear, however, with multimillion-dollar shows such as the Blue Man Group and Phantom: The Las Vegas Spectacular drawing in thousands of guests a month. Other attractions such as celebrity nightclub, Tao, and Madame Tussauds, with its hundred wax celebrity replicas, are two of the hotel's most popular draws. Like most Strip hotels, the Venetian also has convention facilities, but not many are so extensive, including an underground connection to the neighboring 1.2-million-square-foot Sands Expo and Convention Center. A spectacular neighboring property, the Palazzo, opened in December 2007, and is connected to the Venetian via a spectacular octagonal tower.

LEFT: Four members of the Rat Pack pose in front of the Sands Hotel marquee. It was 1960, the year that saw the "Summit at the Sands"—a magical time of entertainment and laughter when Peter Lawford, Frank Sinatra, Sammy Davis Jr., Dean Martin (pictured left to right), and Joey Bishop were filming Ocean's Eleven.

1955

ROYAL NEVADA / STARDUST
While the Riviera survived, the Royal Nevada was a victim of the mid-1950s recession that also claimed the Moulin Rouge

ABOVE: The Royal Nevada opened with great fanfare on April 19, 1955, just one day before the Riviera. Located next to the New Frontier Hotel, the Royal Nevada was billed as the "Showplace of Showtown U.S.A." and featured opera singer Helen Traubel on its opening night. The hotel was also home of the "Dancing Waters," an indoor fountain display composed of thirty-eight tons of cascading water accompanied by colored lights and music. Despite its early promise, the Royal Nevada was plagued with financial problems. Overbuilding on the Strip and a national economic recession resulted in troubles for all of the casinos that opened in the spring of 1955, but only the Royal Nevada completely disappeared. In 1959, it became the Stardust Convention Center.

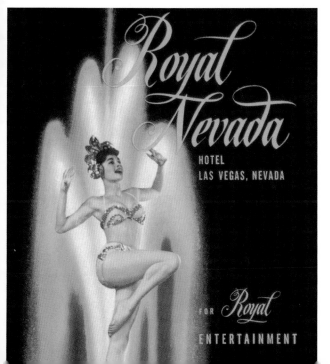

ABOVE: All remnants of the Royal Nevada were destroyed with the implosion of the Stardust in March 2007. The owner, Boyd Gaming Corporation, then began work on its planned $4 billion luxury Echelon Place project in June 2007. The severe economic downtown that affected Las Vegas in 2008 prompted Boyd Gaming to halt construction on the project temporarily that year. Only the steel shell of the Echelon Place construction remains on the site today.

LEFT: An advertisement for the Royal Nevada features a showgirl posed against the "Dancing Waters" that were the hotel's trademark during its short-lived time on the Las Vegas Strip.

1960

STARDUST / ECHELON PLACE

The Stardust was responsible for bringing the first Paris show to Las Vegas

ABOVE: At its opening on July 2, 1958, the $10 million Stardust was one of the largest hotels in Las Vegas, and its distinctive neon sign the largest in the world. The twenty-seven-foot-high sign stretched 217 feet across the front of the resort and could be seen for over three miles. The Stardust was also acclaimed for importing the first French showgirl spectacular—the Lido de Paris—to the Strip. The work of acclaimed show producer Donn Arden, the Lido de Paris was the first Las Vegas show to present nudity in a way that was different from the typical burlesque and striptease shows common to the era. Arden became known for mixing spectacular sets and effects with tasteful and elegant showgirls dressed in the most luxurious fabrics, feathers, sequins, and rhinestones. He was helped in this endeavor by the remarkable stage in the Café Continental showroom, which featured six hydraulic lifts, a swimming tank under the stage,

1958

ABOVE: The look of the Stardust changed greatly over the years with the expansion of its convention space and the addition of a thirty-two-story tower in 1991. This is how it looked in 2005 in the final phase before implosion.

and an ice rink that was stored under the theater seats until needed. His lifelong friend and business partner Margaret Kelly, better known as Madame Bluebell, was responsible for selecting and managing the stunning showgirls who formed the glamorous living backdrop for the showroom stage.

ABOVE: In 1968, the hotel replaced its original neon sign with a 188-foot pylon topped with multicolored stars. The Stardust was dogged by scandal over the years; the book and movie *Casino* were based in large part on Frank "Lefty" Rosenthal's colorful career at the hotel and the money it provided for Chicago crime families. In 1985, the hotel lost its tainted reputation when it became part of the locally owned Boyd Gaming family of properties. The Stardust was yet another casino that fell short of its fiftieth anniversary, closing in November 2006 to make way for what was to be Boyd Gaming's new luxury property development Echelon Place. In typical Las Vegas fashion, the Stardust Hotel was destroyed in a ritual-like implosion complete with celebratory fireworks at 2:33 a.m. on March 13, 2007. Its famous sign was also dismantled and taken to the Neon Boneyard just north of downtown. Construction began on the $4 billion Echelon Place in June 2007, and went on until Las Vegas's unfortunate economic climate led Boyd Gaming to halt construction in August 2008.

1955

ABOVE: The nine-story, 250-room Riviera opened on April 20, 1955, as the first high-rise on the Strip. Built at a cost of $8.5 million, it emphasized European splendor in its decor and was one of the first resorts to utilize elevators. Italian marble and corrugated copper fixtures brought a touch of elegance to the lobby, and individual floors were named after French resort cities such as Nice, Cannes, and Monte Carlo. The Clover Room, the hotel's 10,000-square-foot showroom, was the largest of its kind on the Strip at the time. Opening act Liberace made headlines with his then-unheard-of salary of $50,000 a week, but the original owners went bankrupt just three months after opening, casualties of a glut of casinos opening on the Strip in 1955. A group of men from the Flamingo's management team (including Gus Greenbaum) were offered the chance to take over the hotel soon afterward, and their improvements eventually stabilized the Riviera.

RIVIERA

A north Strip survivor, the Riviera outlasted many of its neighbors

ABOVE: Over the years, the Riviera managed to survive a number of financial downturns. Of the four hotels that opened in the spring of 1955, it is the only survivor. A number of renovations over the years have changed its exterior, but none as dramatically as the erection of this wall-mounted glass display on the casino's facade that features colorful neon lighting and graphic panels. Much of the movie *Casino* was filmed here in 1995. On April 20, 2005, with fireworks off its Monaco Tower, the Riviera celebrated its fiftieth anniversary, making it the fifth Strip property to reach the half-century mark. Despite its longevity, the Riviera has struggled as it moves into its sixth decade. With the demise of its northern Strip neighbors the Stardust, Westward Ho, and the New Frontier, foot traffic for the hotel went down significantly. Despite financial difficulties, the Riviera continues to provide a variety of value-priced entertainment options, and has hosted some of the longest-running shows on the Las Vegas Strip. The water-themed Splash production show, the amusing female impersonators of An Evening at La Cage, and the topless Crazy Girls show have attracted hundreds of thousands of tourists over the years, but the only one of the three that is still running is Crazy Girls, which celebrated its twenty-fifth anniversary in 2012.

LA CONCHA MOTEL
An ordinary building with an extraordinary lobby

BELOW: Designed by renowned African American architect Paul Revere Williams, the La Concha Motel opened in 1961 on the Las Vegas Strip just next to the Riviera. The unique concrete shell-like design of the La Concha lobby was one of the most striking examples of mid-century modern architecture ever constructed in Las Vegas. In 2004, the motel was torn down, and the La Concha lobby was placed on Preserve

1961

Nevada's list of ten most endangered sites. Williams, the first African American member of the American Institute of Architects, was known for his work in Los Angeles designing celebrity homes, with his most famous creation the iconic flying saucerlike building at Los Angeles International Airport. In Las Vegas, Williams has both residential and public works to his credit.

BELOW: In December 2003, La Concha owner and real estate developer Lorenzo Doumani tore down the motel portion of the structure to make way for a planned hotel development. Mindful of the architectural and historical significance of the La Concha lobby, a number of Las Vegas residents worked hard to ensure that Paul Williams's iconic structure would be preserved, and the Doumani family promised the building to the Neon Museum in 2005. Engineers struggled mightily with the logistics of moving the fragile concrete shell to its location near the Neon Boneyard just north of downtown. In 2006, it was cut into sections and transported by truck to its new location at night. The following year it was reassembled and restoration began on the structure in order to prepare it for its role as the visitor center and gift shop for the Neon Museum.

LEFT: The La Concha Motel as it looked shortly after its construction in 1961. The Riviera Hotel and Casino and its parking lot can been seen just north of the La Concha.

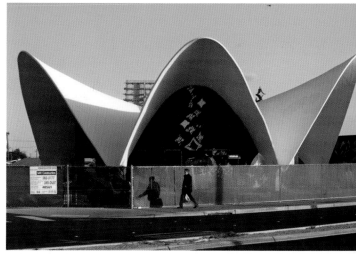

ABOVE: Postcard view of the massive but graceful concrete arches of the La Concha Motel lobby. In its later years, the building was overshadowed by extensions to the Riviera, in particular the wall-mounted neon display that bordered the Strip.

1955

ROOFTOP VIEW FROM THE RIVIERA LOOKING NORTH

In the fourteen years after the El Rancho Vegas opened, the north Strip changed dramatically

LEFT: Marshall Wright, the Riviera's first general manager, shows off the easterly view of the Las Vegas landscape from the rooftop of the newly constructed Riviera Hotel in April 1955. Just behind Wright is the Thunderbird Hotel; traveling north along the Strip to the left is the distinctive windmill of the El Rancho Vegas and still further, and less visible, the Sahara Hotel on the right. The Royal Nevada hotel had opened the previous day just south of the Riviera. Four new major resorts would open that spring, leading *Life* magazine to write the headline "Las Vegas—Is Boom Overextended?" There was some truth to the question, as the Riviera and Dunes immediately experienced financial difficulties, the Moulin Rouge closed later that year, and the Royal Nevada was gone by 1959.

ABOVE: Fifty years later, the view is dramatically different, with both the El Rancho Vegas and the Thunderbird Hotel gone. The 1,149-foot-tall Stratosphere Tower, which calls itself "the tallest building west of the Mississippi River and tallest freestanding observation tower in the U.S." has dominated the Strip skyline since its opening in April 1996. In the early twenty-first century, however, competition from the neighboring high-rises of the Sky Las Vegas condominium and Hilton Grand Vacation Suites, as well as the unfinished towers of the failed Fontainebleau Resort, have made its towering appearance a little less impressive. Interestingly, the Stratosphere is not physically considered a part of the Strip, as its location just north of Sahara Avenue places it firmly within downtown Las Vegas.

1955

DUNES HOTEL / BELLAGIO

Showgirls helped rescue the struggling Dunes
in 1957

ABOVE: This thirty-foot fiberglass sultan atop the casino
entrance greeted visitors to the Dunes Hotel when it opened
on May 23, 1955. Like most early Las Vegas Strip hotels, the
Dunes consisted of low- or mid-rise buildings, and cars parked
directly in front of the casino. Unfortunately, inexperienced
management and competition from a glut of hotels that opened
in the spring of 1955 quickly led the Dunes into financial
difficulties. The property struggled until manager Major
Arteburn Riddle took over in late 1956. That same year,
legendary jazz singer Billie Holiday made her one and only
Las Vegas appearance in the Dunes showroom. In 1957, in an
attempt to reinvigorate the hotel, Riddle added a number of

BELOW: Blonde bombshell Jayne Mansfield (dressed in red) appears more concerned with looking glamorous than playing roulette in this publicity shot for the Dunes Hotel and Casino in 1955.

1955

attractions, beginning with Minsky's Follies, the first topless revue in Las Vegas. Riddle continued his string of innovations in 1961 by opening the elegant Sultan's Table, considered by some to be the first true gourmet restaurant on the Las Vegas Strip, with Arturo Romero's Magic Violins providing the entertainment. That same year, Riddle brought Frederic Apcar's Vive Les Girls, a miniproduction revue, to the hotel's Persian Room. One of the most expensive lounge shows in Las Vegas history, it was an immediate success, and ran for many years. In 1963, Riddle added to the Dunes's entertainment lineup in a spectacular way when he imported the French extravaganza Casino de Paris. Directed by producer Frederic Apcar, the show was presented in the Dunes showroom on its famous multilevel stage and featured extravagant and expensive costumes designed by Jose Luis Vinas.

ABOVE: In October 1993, the Dunes Hotel was imploded in a torrent of dust and debris to make way for casino mogul Steve Wynn's Bellagio resort. Modeled after a Tuscan village and constructed at a cost of over $1 billion, the Bellagio celebrated its grand opening on October 15, 1998. An 8.5-acre artificial lake fronts Las Vegas Boulevard and a botanical garden and spectacular blown-glass ceiling by artist Dale Chihuly are among the most distinctive interior features. In 2004, the Bellagio unveiled over 900 additional rooms, new retail stores, more restaurants, and 60,000 extra feet of exhibition space. The Bellagio's lovely Conservatory and Botanical Gardens, just past the lobby, are one of the most popular free attractions on the Strip and regularly attract both tourists and locals. The gardens change with the seasons, and a staff of 140 expert horticulturists maintain the freshness of the hundreds of plants and flowers, in addition to incorporating water features and attractions such as a butterfly gallery, gazebo, and Ferris wheel.

DUNES HOTEL / BELLAGIO

The 180-foot Dunes pylon made way for a spectacular fountain show

ABOVE: An aerial view of the Dunes hotel as it looked around 1967 just after the completion of Caesars Palace to the north, and prior to the destruction of the Flamingo's neon bubble tower in 1968. The 180-foot neon pylon just in front of the hotel was added to the Dunes in 1964, and was the tallest freestanding sign in the world at the time. Designed by Lee Klay of Federal Sign in Los Angeles, the $500,000 sign provoked complaints from hotel guests who were disturbed by the red glow given off by the three miles of neon tubing. As a result, the hotel was forced to line the window drapes of those rooms that faced the sign. The twenty-four-story high-rise, which opened on July 15, 1965, stands in stark contrast to the low-rise rooms in the background. Yet another innovation by Dunes general manager Major Riddle, the new tower added 250 rooms to the hotel's inventory, and was home to the Top O' the Strip restaurant, a nursery for the children of visiting guests, and a shopping arcade

ABOVE: An aerial view of the lake at the Bellagio shows the outline of the fountain mechanisms that can shoot water up to 500 feet in the air. More than a thousand fountains make up the display, which entertains millions of visitors each year. Spectators gather around the perimeter to watch the spectacle, and passing cars even stop Strip traffic in their quest to see the show. The water spouts and sways to synchronized light and music and was featured as the end of the 2001 movie Ocean's

Eleven. In December 2011, for the first time in six years, three new songs were added to the repertoire of the Bellagio fountains: the Beatles' "Lucy in the Sky with Diamonds," Michael Jackson's "Billie Jean," and the Glenn Miller classic "In the Mood." The California-based design firm WET choreographed the new pieces, and in the background, a team of thirty work diligently to ensure that the popular attraction is maintained in tip-top shape.

1966

CAESARS PALACE

The spiritual home of the big fight in Las Vegas—boxer Joe Louis had a role in the casino

ABOVE: A monument to Las Vegas excess and the work of casino visionary Jay Sarno, Caesars Palace celebrated its grand opening on August 5, 1966, with a party that topped $1 million. Its distinctive Greco-Roman design by architect Melvin Grossman included eighteen huge fountains, a 135-foot driveway lined with imported Italian cypress trees, and more than $150,000 worth of imported marble statuary from Italy. Complimenting the hotel's fourteen-story high-rise was the 980-seat Circus Maximus showroom, which was based on the Colosseum in Rome. The first production show to appear at the hotel was the appropriately titled Rome Swings with headliner Andy Williams. The hotel also made its mark with a number of distinctive culinary establishments that were the work of noted chef and restaurateur Nat Hart. Among these restaurants was the celebrated Bacchanal Room, where patrons were treated to a meal served by waitresses dressed in Roman-style togas.

BELOW: This parking lot at Caesars Palace was the scene of one of the worst floods in Las Vegas history on July 3, 1975, when some 700 cars were inundated after a heavy thunderstorm that resulted in massive runoff from the Flamingo Wash, north of the hotel.

1970

ABOVE: Although the replica of the Winged Victory of Samothrace continues to greet visitors to Caesars Palace, much of the hotel's exterior has changed dramatically. Between 1970 and 1979, three high-rises joined the original tower, and the twenty-six-story Palace Tower was added in 1997. As Caesars Palace moves into its fifth decade as a Strip stalwart, the property's appearance has continued to change and grow with the times, all the while managing to keep up its trademark Greco-Roman theme. After the closing of the original Circus Maximus showroom in 2000, the Colosseum was custom-built for singer Céline Dion and her show A New Day. The addition of the Octavius Tower in January 2012 added another 668 rooms to the hotel, raising the property's total room count to 4,000. The hotel continues to be a haven for fine dining aficionados.

1976

LAS VEGAS STRIP LOOKING NORTH AT NIGHT

As buildings have risen on the Strip, so has the scale of their marquees

LEFT: A glittering view of Las Vegas Boulevard at night looking north from its intersection with Flamingo in the early 1970s. The Sands tower is visible with the striped Circus Circus big top to the right. Among the neon signs that glow along the Strip is the Caesars Palace marquee with its trademark Greco-Roman design. Three major neon sign companies, YESCO

ABOVE: Some thirty years later, the Caesars Palace marquee still figures prominently in the Strip's landscape, but a series of high-rises and signs has altered the skyline. The Mirage and its neighbor, the thirty-six-story, pirate-themed Treasure Island resort, loom in the distance. Across the way on the east side of the Strip, a portion of the Flamingo's dramatic wraparound advertisement on the front of the hotel is prominent. Next to it, peeping into view in the distance, are the tops of the Imperial Palace, Harrah's, and the Venetian. In 2009, Harrah's (now Caesars) Entertainment announced plans for Project Linq. Unlike a typical Strip construction project, it will not involve building a new casino, but rather the construction of an entertainment corridor of bars, restaurants, and shops that

1957

HACIENDA / MANDALAY BAY

The hotel that ran its own airline

1965

ABOVE: Like most Strip hotels from the 1940s to the 1970s, the Hacienda's parking lot was located in front of the hotel just off Las Vegas Boulevard. It was a far cry from the multistory parking garages of today's Mandalay Bay and THE Hotel. The family emphasis changed over the years, as witnessed by the marquee of the 1965 photograph (top), which advertised "Burlesque Dancing" and "Topless Models."

LEFT: In June 1956, Warren "Doc" Bayley's Hacienda Hotel opened on the far south end of the Strip, with its trademark neon horseback rider welcoming visitors to the $6 million resort. Difficulties in obtaining a gaming license meant that the resort opened without a casino, and its isolated location, almost two miles from the nearest hotel, made the Hacienda's survival difficult. In October 1956, the resort finally received its gaming license and the casino opened, saving the Hacienda from certain decline. Despite the challenges posed by the remote location. It succeeded by sponsoring family-oriented attractions and introducing an air fleet to ferry passengers in from California and other U.S. cities. On December 28, 1964, Bayley's unexpected death flung his widow Judy Bayley into the spotlight, and she eagerly rose to the challenge of running the Hacienda—the first woman to run a hotel-casino. Judy Bayley was a generous philanthropist who did much to support the Las Vegas community before cancer claimed her on December 31, 1971.

RIGHT: Imploded on New Year's Eve 1996, the Hacienda was replaced by Mandalay Bay, a luxury resort styled after an exotic South Seas island, which opened on March 3, 1999. Landscaped with over 5,000 palm trees, the resort also features a sand beach with a unique wave pool that allows for adjustable waves. In October 2003, the hotel added 100,000 square feet of upscale shopping space in an arcade sky bridge spanning the street that separates Mandalay Bay from the Luxor. In late December 2003, Mandalay Bay added a second forty-three-story tower known as THE Hotel with over 1,100 suites. This will be transformed into the Delano Las Vegas by the end of 2013.

1957

TROPICANA HOTEL
Home to the Folies Bergère for almost fifty years

ABOVE: A striking sixty-foot tulip-shaped fountain was just one of the Tropicana's distinctive features when it opened on the Strip's barren south end on April 4, 1957. Built at a cost of $15 million, the 300-room Caribbean-themed resort was nicknamed the "Tiffany's of the Strip" for its elegant design and luxurious surroundings. At its opening, singer Eddie Fisher headlined Monte Prosser's popular Tropicana Revue in the elegant Theatre Restaurant in front of a star-studded crowd. Alexander Perino, executive supervisor of cuisine, brought fine dining to the Tropicana. In December 1959, the Tropicana became home to the Strip's second French showgirl spectacular when entertainment director Lou Walters (father of Barbara) brought the Folies Bergère directly from Paris to the hotel's showroom. It soon became one of the most popular attractions at the hotel. Like many Strip hotels, the Tropicana's luster faded over the years, and as its ownership changed, the hotel became the site of a notorious mob skim operation in the 1970s.

RIGHT: The Tropicana's trademark fountain fell victim to the wrecking ball when the hotel was remodeled in the late 1970s. The hotel's first high-rise, the twenty-two-story Tiffany Tower, was completed in 1979. In 1985, the "Island of Las Vegas" theme was unveiled, and resulted in the addition of a five-acre water oasis and another high-rise. The Tropicana has gone through a series of corporate ownership changes in recent years. In July 2009, the Tropicana emerged from bankruptcy protection and was taken over by ONEX Corporation. Under its new ownership, the Tropicana underwent a multistage renovation in a South Beach style that accounts for the new white look of the existing towers, sleek new room decor with plantation shutters, and a remake of the casino with white floors, columns, and chairs. Another significant change occurred in the Tropicana showroom when the Folies Bergère closed in March 2009 just a few months short of its fiftieth anniversary at the hotel. The Tropicana is now home to the unique and colorful Mob Attraction Las Vegas, an interactive exhibit featuring 3-D holograms of famous mob-movie icons and artifacts.

BELOW: The lush landscaping that surrounded the Tropicana Hotel and Casino and gave it its Caribbean feel can be seen in this image of the casino atrium.

Castaways

HOTEL
Casino
restaurant

WORLD'S BIGGEST
POKER KENO!

Grog L'Treasure Shoppe DISCOUNT
LIQUORS

1972

LEFT: This small Polynesian-themed casino hotel, located directly across the street from the Sands, billed itself as a "private island in the center of the Strip." It had originally opened as the Sans Souci in October 1957, but changed its name to the Castaways in 1964, and became known for its jewel-like, two-story honeymoon suites. The Polynesian theme continued throughout the hotel with its Kon Tiki Lounge and the tempting Pagoda Pool surrounded by swaying palms. Toward the back of the photo is the fourteen-ton teakwood "Gateway to Luck" replica of the Jain temple at Palitana, India. The replica was carved by sixty-five artisans for the 1904 St. Louis

ABOVE: The Castaways closed in July 1987 to make way for the construction of Steve Wynn's Mirage. The luxury hotel—with its shimmering, Y-shaped golden tower—opened in November 1989 and is credited with starting the building renaissance that reinvigorated Las Vegas in the 1990s. Neon is noticeably absent from the Mirage's design, replaced by more tangible attractions such as the flaming volcano and Siegfried and Roy's Secret Garden and Dolphin Habitat. Since the departure of Siegfried and Roy's iconic magic show in 2003, the Mirage has boasted many high-profile acts, including a Cirque du Soleil show and the Beatles-themed LOVE. The hotel's trademark volcano

MGM GRAND HOTEL / BALLYS

Home to the last remaining showgirl extravaganza on the Strip

BELOW: Built by billionaire Kirk Kerkorian at a cost of $106 million, the twenty-six-story MGM Grand opened on December 5, 1973. With 2,100 rooms and an interior decor patterned on the film *Grand Hotel*, the MGM Grand brought large-scale class and elegance to the Strip. Five restaurants, two showrooms, and a jai alai court completed the hotel's luxurious amenities. The first show to open in the Ziegfeld Room that year was Donn Arden's spectacular Hallelujah Hollywood. On the morning of November 21, 1980, an electrical fire broke out in the hotel's kitchen, killing eighty-five people. Arden, in rehearsals for his new production show Jubilee!, narrowly escaped.

1980

ABOVE: Helicopters hover over the smoke-filled MGM Grand Hotel and Casino as part of the rescue effort that plucked hundreds of guests off the roof of the hotel during the fire on November 21, 1980. The tragic loss of life spurred massive lawsuits against a total of 118 companies, including the MGM Grand. A $223 million settlement fund was distributed to the victims and their families within three years of the fire.

BELOW: As a result of the MGM Grand tragedy, fire safety laws and building codes were changed around the country. The hotel was totally rebuilt, and in 1986, it was sold to the Bally Entertainment Corporation, which constructed a distinctive twirling neon spiral walkway out front in 1994. Lacking a major theme to compete with the newer megaresorts, Bally's cultivates an aura of old-time Vegas style and glamour with its slogan, "Real. Live. Las Vegas." In July 2011, the Donn Arden production Jubilee! celebrated its thirtieth anniversary at the hotel, and is the last remaining showgirl spectacular on the Las Vegas Strip following the closure of the Folies Bergère in 2009. The show might be something of a throwback in the days of Cirque-style acrobats and contortionists, but its brand of kitsch continues to attract audiences in search of old-time Vegas entertainment. A new MGM Grand, also developed by Kerkorian, opened in 1993 on the northeast corner of Tropicana and Las Vegas Boulevard. At its opening, it was the largest hotel in the world, but it now ranks third.

1976

ALADDIN / PLANET HOLLYWOOD

From Aladdin's Lamp to Hollywood neon in a few short years

ABOVE: This is the second version of the Aladdin as it looked shortly after its completion in June 1976 following a $60 million renovation. The original version of the Aladdin, built by former Sahara owner Milton Prell, opened April 1, 1966, on the site of the failed Tally Ho Resort. The Arabian-themed resort became famous as the site of Elvis Presley's wedding in May 1967 and gained notoriety when alleged ties to Midwest mobsters led Nevada gaming officials to briefly close the casino on August 6, 1979. The Aladdin sign shown here was a stylized, scroll-topped pylon designed by YESCO that featured a revolving three-sided marquee topped with an illuminated Aladdin's lamp. Its unique design led to its inclusion in the pages of the prestigious *Art in America* magazine.

RIGHT: On April 27, 1998, the second version of the Aladdin was removed to make way for a luxurious new Aladdin Hotel and Casino with expanded retail and entertainment facilities. The new version (pictured right) opened in August 2000, its outer facade framed by palm trees and styled after a Moorish castle with its interior hosting the 500,000-square foot Desert Passage shopping center. Sadly, the hotel was plagued with problems from its opening, and elements of the resort's design attracted criticism early on. Even more damaging was the fact that its owner and primary investor could not meet his loan commitments. Less than three years after its opening, the hotel was sold in bankruptcy on June 20, 2003, to a partnership of Planet Hollywood and Starwood Hotels & Resorts Worldwide. The resort's new owners slowly transformed the *Arabian Nights*–themed Aladdin in stages into the ultra-modern Planet Hollywood resort with a facade characterized by brightly colored neon, digital signage, and texturized bubbles. The Desert Passage was transformed into the Hollywood-themed Miracle Mile Shops, the casino expanded, and new restaurants and a nightclub were also added. On April 17, 2007, the former Aladdin officially opened as the Planet Hollywood Resort and Casino, and in February 2010, it became part of the Caesars Entertainment empire.

Las Vegas, Nevada "Where the Fun Begins . . . and Never Ends"

LEFT: This postcard promoted the Aladdin, but the mock Tudor architecture of the buildings tells a story. They were adapted from the Henry VIII-themed Tally Ho which opened on New Year's Eve 1964 but closed within six months.

1998

BOARDWALK / CITY CENTER

The Boardwalk development didn't last long before it was replaced by Vegas's own leaning towers

ABOVE: The Boardwalk Hotel Casino opened in 1994 on the site of the former Viscount Hotel. It was characterized by a faux Coney Island facade that featured both a nonoperating roller coaster and a Ferris wheel. Its most distinctive feature, however, was a giant clown face visible during the day that might alternately bring a laugh or a twinge of fear to passersby. Although dwarfed by its neighbors the Bellagio and the Monte Carlo, the hotel provided value-priced accommodation for tourists, and for many years, the casino boasted a Prince impersonator in its small showroom. Its twenty-four-hour Surf Buffet was once promoted by Eric "Butterbean" Esch, a heavyweight boxer and professional wrestler.

ABOVE: On January 9, 2006, the Boardwalk was among several businesses closed to make way for the MGM Mirage's City Center development. Construction on the $9.2 billion resort began in June 2006. Although the initial planning and construction of the massive development took place at a time of unbridled growth in Las Vegas, the challenging economic climate that affected most of the country from 2008 onward meant that its building was plagued with financial troubles. At its grand opening in December 2009, City Center included the Aria Hotel and Casino, Mandarin Oriental Hotel, Vdara Hotel and Spa, and the high-end Crystals Shopping Center. The Veer

Towers, unique twin condominium towers that lean in opposite directions, opened in July 2010. A spectacular collection of outdoor sculptures add to the Manhattan-like feel of the development, which covers some seventy-six acres. The Harmon high-rise is the only major blight on the City Center development; construction defects discovered in 2008 reduced its tower from a planned forty-nine stories to a mere twenty-eight, and it has never opened. As of 2012, the property's owner, MGM Resorts International, has been seeking the court's permission to implode the Harmon, against the wishes of the tower's contractor, Perini Building Co.

INTERNATIONAL / LAS VEGAS HOTEL AND CASINO

The hotel inextricably linked with Elvis Presley

LEFT: The International, acclaimed as the largest hotel and casino in the world at its opening on July 3, 1969, was the second hotel constructed off the Strip on Paradise Road. The brainchild of developer and financier Kirk Kerkorian, the thirty-story, 1,500-room International was designed by architect Martin Stern. The original 139-foot tripodic sign and marquee shown here was deliberately designed to reflect the shape of the hotel and was the brainchild of Bob Miller from the sign company AD-ART. But it was the hotel's entertainment lineup that really put the International on the map, starting with Barbra Streisand, who headlined the opening. Elvis Presley continued where Streisand left off with his first performance on July 31, 1969, packing crowds into the 2,000-seat showroom. He continued to perform for the International as it made its transition into the Las Vegas Hilton until 1976. The International and the Flamingo became part of the Hilton hotel chain in July 1970, when Kerkorian sold them and used the profits to build an even grander hotel—the MGM.

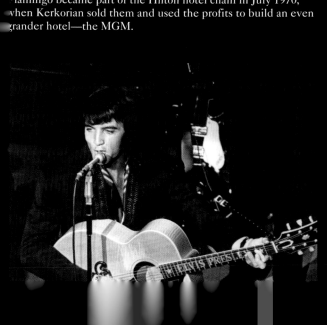

ABOVE: From 1970 to 2011, the magnificent towers of the Las Vegas Hilton reigned supreme over Paradise Road. In recognition of Elvis's seven years of sold-out shows at the hotel, the Hilton erected a bronze statue of the famous entertainer outside the showroom in 1978, a year after his death. In February 1981, just months after the tragic MGM Grand fire on the Strip, the Las Vegas Hilton was the site of an arson fire that claimed eight lives. Although this was a sad episode in the Hilton's history, the hotel continued to flourish, and in 1986, it opened the largest race and sports book in the country. Following Barbra Streisand and Elvis, the most recent longtime headliner in the hotel's showroom was Barry Manilow, who appeared at the hotel from 2004 to 2009. It ceased to be a part of the Hilton franchise on January 1, 2012. A few days later, the Las Vegas Hilton changed its name to the LVH—Las Vegas Hotel and Casino, and the lettering was taken down from the iconic gold sign that towers over the property.

LAS VEGAS CONVENTION CENTER
Its flying saucer design was the epitome of Space Age architecture

1959

WORLD CONGRESS OF FLIGHT

LAS VEGAS CONVENTION CENTER

ABOVE: The dome of the Las Vegas Convention Center was its most distinctive feature until it was torn down in 1990.

LEFT: With its modern, Space Age look, the sleek and streamlined Las Vegas Convention Center was the perfect choice to host the World Congress of Flight at its opening on April 12, 1959. Operating under the motto "So far ahead it will always be new," the $5 million Las Vegas Convention Center, with its 119,000 square feet of ground-floor exhibit space, was heavily promoted for its modern features, which included seventeen meeting rooms, soundproof partitions, and the latest electronic communication and control devices such as closed-circuit TV. Promotional material for the new convention center boasted of its proximity to tourist attractions like Lake Mead, Mount Charleston, Hoover Dam, and the star-studded shows on the Las Vegas Strip. Not surprisingly, an even greater selling point for the convention center was the sunny Las Vegas weather that was described in a promotional brochure rather exuberantly as "the healthiest climate anywhere in America." Perhaps one of the lesser-known amenities of the Las Vegas Convention Center at this time was the Las Vegas News Bureau (founded as the Desert Sea News Bureau in 1949), which boasted a large staff of photographers assigned to capture all manner of people, buildings, and events on the Strip in an effort to visually document and promote the city in newspapers and magazines throughout the United States and the world.

BELOW: The Las Vegas Convention Center's adage "So far ahead it will always be new" proved true for only about three decades. The Las Vegas Convention and Visitors Authority (LVCVA) was largely responsible for creating a thriving convention business for Las Vegas. As a result, a rapidly expanding convention industry caught up with the structure by its thirtieth anniversary in 1989. In 1990, the sleek dome was torn down, and an expansion added some 1.6 million square feet of space to the convention center. Two additional expansions in 1998 and 2002 have significantly enlarged the Las Vegas Convention Center, and it now features some 3.2 million square feet of space. Known as the South Hall, a portion of this expansion crosses over Desert Inn Road, and there are four bridges that connect the facilities. Today the mammoth convention center provides space and facilities for a large number of the thousands of conventions held in Las Vegas annually. In 2009, a collection of Vegas memorabilia was buried in a time capsule to be dug up in 2059.

1970

LANDMARK HOTEL

The Landmark made a fitting Space Age
neighbor to the futuristic dome of the
convention center

ABOVE: One of the most distinctive hotel-casinos ever built in
Las Vegas, the Landmark was the dream of one man, Frank
Carrol, who struggled for years to finance its construction. He
broke ground at the corner of Paradise and Convention Center
Drive in 1961, and immediately set about trying to make his
tower the tallest in Las Vegas, engaging in a heated competition
with the Mint Hotel builders, who were constructing their own
high-rise on Fremont Street at the time. In 1962, construction
came to a halt when Carrol was denied financing, and it was
not until he received a $5.5 million loan in 1966 that he was
able to continue construction. Yet even this $5.5 million was not
enough, and in late 1968, billionaire Howard Hughes stepped in

ABOVE: The Landmark's outdoor glass elevator, which took patrons to its casino and nightclub on the twenty-seventh floor, is visible in this color postcard.

ABOVE: The Landmark Hotel's construction was the result of years of financial struggle for its original owner, and those difficulties continued to plague the hotel after its completion. A series of owners struggled to make the property profitable, and in August 1985, owner William "Wildcat" Morris placed the Landmark into Chapter 11 bankruptcy protection. The Landmark closed its doors on August 7, 1990, and its fate remained uncertain before it was purchased by the LVCVA in September 1993 for $15.1 million. On November 7, 1995, movie crews filmed the implosion of the troubled hotel by Controlled Demolition Inc. for use in the film *Mars Attacks!* It now serves as a parking lot for the Las Vegas Convention Center. Today, on the corner where the Landmark's iconic tower once stood, there is a small pink building, the Las Vegas Visitor Information Center. A small but shining legacy to the Landmark Hotel can be found in the portion of the hotel's neon sign that was later placed just north of the information center facing Paradise Road.

to purchase the hotel from Carrol as part of his Vegas hotel-buying spree. After spending a few more million to finalize its construction, Hughes opened the Landmark on July 2, 1969, just overlapping with the grand opening of the International down the street. The hotel contained 525 rooms, some in the shaft of the tower and others in surrounding buildings, as well as a casino and showroom. The three-story glass-and-metal dome at the top housed another casino, lounge, nightclub, and restaurants—all with a 360-degree view of the Las Vegas landscape. The hotel's showroom hosted dozens of big-name stars in its early years, and even had its own production show, Frederic Apcar's Bare Touch of Vegas.

c. 1955

MOULIN ROUGE

Las Vegas's first interracial casino was a failure despite a promising start

ABOVE: Frequently referred to as the "Mississippi of the West," Las Vegas was a deeply segregated town in the 1940s and 1950s. Black patrons were not allowed to enter most casinos on Fremont Street or the Strip, and black entertainers were often refused accommodation at the luxurious resorts where they performed. In May 1955, the elegant Moulin Rouge on Bonanza Road opened as the first interracial casino hotel in Las Vegas, and the first hotel to open in a predominantly residential area. Its design was based on the Moulin Rouge in Paris, and French influences could be seen everywhere—from the stylized Eiffel Tower design on the hotel's casino chips to the showroom murals inspired by Toulouse-Lautrec, and the

ABOVE: A month after the hotel opened, dancers from its revue, the Tropi-Can-Can, graced the cover of *Life* magazine.

BELOW: Despite its initial success and popularity, the Moulin Rouge closed after only six months due to financial mismanagement. Although it was entered on the National Register of Historic Places in December 1992, subsequent owners met with little success in returning it to its former glory. In April 2002, Preserve Nevada added the hotel to its list of the state's eleven most endangered historical sites. Shortly afterward, in May 2003, a fire engulfed and destroyed all but the neon sign, the hotel's facade, and part of the apartments that formed the historic building. In April 2009, the neon script lettering that spelled out Moulin Rouge in front of the hotel was transferred to the Neon Boneyard. Sadly, in June 2010 the Las Vegas Historic Preservation Commission approved the owner's permits to demolish the remaining fire-damaged structures.

security officers wearing uniforms resembling those worn by the French Foreign Legion. The Moulin Rouge appeared to be poised for a successful future. Its line of showgirls performed routines designed by the noted black choreographer Clarence Robinson, known for his work on the Lena Horne film *Stormy Weather*. Entertainers, both black and white, flocked to the hotel's lounge for jam sessions in the early hours of the morning after they had performed for Strip patrons, and the hotel added a third show of its revue at 2:30 a.m. to accommodate the crowds. But then, just as suddenly as it had exploded on the Las Vegas scene, the Moulin Rouge closed, declaring bankruptcy in December 1955.

1954

SHOWBOAT / CASTAWAYS
Unlike Ol' Man River, the Showboat failed to keep rolling along

2005

LEFT: Las Vegas residents "Mom" and "Pop" Squires christen the new Showboat Hotel on its opening day, September 3, 1954. Built at a cost of $2 million, the nautically themed hotel was designed to resemble an 1840s side-wheeler, with its prow jutting out into the swimming pool. Its designers had taken inspiration from the recently released movie musical *Showboat*, and as a result, the hotel featured nautical themes such as portholes and hand-painted ceiling sconces. Its location near the remote intersection of Fremont and Boulder Highway was carefully planned after contemporary surveys suggested that this area would soon be the new center of town. This assumption turned out to be false. The hotel's management tried various promotions as a means to lure customers, including a 49¢ breakfast and sponsoring giveaways of prizes ranging from televisions to appliances and cars. Its greatest success came when the Showboat's management added a twenty-four-lane bowling alley to the hotel in 1959, and it soon became the scene of numerous professional bowling tournaments in the 1960s and 1970s. By 1979, the Showboat had 106 lanes and was the third-largest bowling center in America.

ABOVE: Its original Showboat exterior long gone, the resort was sold and reopened as Castaways in 2001. Things did not go well for the second generation. By 2003, Castaways had generated more than $50 million in debt and was soon in bankruptcy. Station Casinos bought the twenty-six-acre site for $33.7 million in 2006, and the Castaways tower was imploded in that same year. The site currently sits vacant (below).

1963

LAS VEGAS SIGN LOOKING NORTH

Betty Willis's fabulous gift to Las Vegas

LEFT: A view of the "Welcome to Fabulous Las Vegas" sign looking north on the Strip in 1969 shows a background of billboards and tiny motels in the distance. One of the most recognizable symbols of Las Vegas, the twenty-five-foot sign was designed by commercial artist Betty Willis and created by Western Electric Display in 1959. The starburst at the top is typical of the Googie design style that came out of the Atomic Age in the mid-twentieth century. At the time of the sign's construction, there was no Interstate 15, and all traffic from Los Angeles traveled into Las Vegas along Highway 91, which had become better known as the Las Vegas Strip by then. Its placement on the far southern portion of the Strip past the Hacienda Hotel (actually four miles outside of the Las Vegas city limits) ensured that all visitors who drove in and out of Las Vegas on their way to Los Angeles would see the colorful sign. Willis, a Las Vegas native who continued to design signs until she retired at the age of seventy-seven, never copyrighted the sign's design, noting later that it was her gift to the city. The sign's image can be found today on all kinds of Las Vegas souvenirs.

RIGHT: The "Welcome to Fabulous Las Vegas Nevada" sign looks the same today, but the backdrop on the Strip has changed dramatically. In the distance, a vista of high-rises and palm trees populate Las Vegas Boulevard where low-rise hotels, billboards, and desert once reigned supreme. The sign itself has become such a Las Vegas icon that it was chosen to adorn the city's official centennial license plate and is featured on the "Welcome to Nevada" U.S. postage stamp. Its prominence as a symbol of Las Vegas has also led to the placement of smaller versions of the sign in other parts of town, with one perched on the north end of Las Vegas Boulevard as it heads into downtown, and another on Boulder Highway just north of Tropicana Avenue. To accommodate the constant stream of tourists who stop to take photographs in front of the iconic sign, the county constructed an island and parking lot around it in 2008. Nominated for a listing on the National Register of Historic Places in March 2009 by Clark County, the sign's listing was approved in May of that year.

SHOWGIRLS
A dying art in Las Vegas

The epitome of glamour and sex appeal, the showgirl has long been a fixture in Las Vegas entertainment. Early Strip hotels such as the El Rancho, Last Frontier, and Desert Inn had chorus lines, but it was the arrival of the Stardust's spectacular French import Lido de Paris in 1958 that made them a central part of the casinos' entertainment strategy. It was followed in quick succession by two additional French production shows, the Tropicana's Folies Bergère in 1959 and Casino de Paris, which opened at the Dunes in 1963. These shows and many others that followed through the 1990s made the showgirl a highly desirable profession in Las Vegas. Although the

LEFT: In this 1978 photo from the opening number of the Stardust's Allez Lido, the principal dancer poses amid a sea of feathers, fur, and sequins.

layperson may not realize it, there has always been a difference
between "showgirls" and "dancers" in Las Vegas productions.
Dancers were generally covered or "dressed" and performed
more complicated dance moves, whereas showgirls were
typically topless (or "nude" in the production show vernacular)
and, because of their elaborate and often heavy costumes and
headdresses, were limited to moving elegantly across the stage
rather than actively dancing. Although both dancers and
showgirls have always had height requirements—the latter
typically required applicants be in the five foot nine to six foot
range, if only to make their elaborate costumes stand out on
the huge stages of the Las Vegas showrooms. Over the years,
the Las Vegas production show, with its elegant feathered and
sequined showgirls, has slowly been overtaken by other types
of entertainment, such as Cirque du Soleil, that feature acrobats
and gymnasts. With the closure of the Folies Bergère in 2009,
only Jubilee! remains as an example of the classic showgirl
production in Las Vegas.

LEFT: Three showgirls from Donn Arden's long-running show Jubilee!
strut their stuff onstage at Bally's. The show celebrated its thirtieth
anniversary on the Strip in July 2011.

BELOW: A line of girls from La Nouvelle Eve grace the stage of the
El Rancho Vegas Hotel and Casino in 1959, just a year before a fire
destroyed the hotel.

ABOVE: The Copa Girls entrance an audience in the Copa Room at the
Sands shortly after it opened in December 1952.

BELOW: The beautiful but modest attire of these dancers onstage in the
Dunes Hotel and Casino in 1955 contrasts strongly with the far more
scantily clad showgirls of today.

c.1949

SLOTS
No longer a nickel-and-dime operation

As table games were the real moneymaker for casinos in Las Vegas's early days, slot machines were generally accorded secondary status—a distraction for the wives of men engaged in "serious gambling." The "one-armed bandits" were three-reeled mechanical slot machines, far removed from the digital marvels of today's casinos. In the 1930s, it was typical for most of the small clubs on Fremont Street to purchase their machines from the Mills Novelty Company. This tradition continued into the 1950s, with the Mills High Tops nickel and quarter machines being the favorite choices of the downtown casinos. Mills machines also dominated the Las Vegas Strip in its early days, until they were largely replaced by the brightly lit machines of the Jennings Manufacturing Company. On both the Strip and Fremont Street, this dominance ended in the late 1960s when Bally machines, a latecomer to the slot machine business, procured a virtual monopoly in Las Vegas with their revolutionary new machines that used electromechanical circuitry, multiple coin play, and a payout unit that could dispense many different pays in various amounts.

LEFT: A typical Jennings slot machine, personalized for the Sands Hotel from the 1950s, is representative of the "one-armed bandits" that made Las Vegas famous.

RIGHT: Western-themed attire was a common sight in Las Vegas casinos. The motto "Come as you are" is exemplified by this woman playing slots during a war bond rally in September 1943.

ABOVE: A view of the Sands casino in the early 1960s shows a small bank of slot machines played primarily by well-dressed women in evening attire.

RIGHT: Paul McCartney tries his hand at the slots during the Beatles' brief stay in Las Vegas just before their appearance at the convention center on August 20, 1964.

BELOW: A striking contrast to the earlier image of patrons at the Sands, this shows the vast difference in both the dress code and the design of slot machines in Las Vegas today.

1952

McCARRAN FIELD / INTERNATIONAL

Named in honor of Nevada's longtime U.S. senator Patrick McCarran

ABOVE AND RIGHT: Las Vegas residents throng Rockwell Field, the second airfield in Las Vegas, as a Western Air Express plane inaugurating regular contract airmail service to the city arrived on April 17, 1926. In 1930, Western Air Express moved to a new airfield when Rockwell Field closed. After World War II, Clark County began a search for an airport that could service commercial air traffic for the expanding town. George Crockett's Alamo Field, located on Highway 91, four miles south of the city of Las Vegas, was selected, and on December 19, 1948, the new airport was given the name McCarran Field in honor of Nevada's longtime U.S. senator Patrick McCarran. Initially it was serviced by just four airlines, including the planes of TWA and Western Air Express (shown above).

BELOW: The stone pillars with propellers that marked the entrance to the original McCarran Field were moved to the new airport in 1950. They have remained just off of south Las Vegas Boulevard ever since.

McCarran Field, Las Vegas, Nevada

ABOVE: As the number of Las Vegas hotel-casinos increased in the 1950s, there was a corresponding increase in tourists, and Las Vegas became ever more reliant on air travel. Additional airlines were soon crowding each other for space, and a number of expansions occurred during the airport's first decade. Even those proved inadequate by 1959, however. Planning then began on a new terminal situated on the east side of the airfield, just opposite the original terminal. It opened in March 1963, and in 1968, McCarran was officially renamed McCarran International Airport. Continued growth expanded the airport in the 1970s with the construction of the A and B gates, and then into 1980s and 1990s with the addition of the C and D gates. In 2011, year-end statistics for McCarran Airport revealed that the facility serviced a staggering 41,479,814 passengers; these numbers are sure to grow with the opening of Terminal 3 in June 2012, which will service all international flights and a number of domestic airlines as well. Statistics released by Airports Council International in 2011 listed McCarran International Airport as the nineteenth-busiest airport in the world by passenger traffic.

1923

TOMIYASU FARM
Pioneering Japanese-American farmer who made the desert bloom

ABOVE: Far from the bustle of Fremont Street and the Strip, the 160-acre Tomiyasu farm flourished in the vicinity of what is now Pecos and Warm Springs Road from the 1920s to the 1960s. Owner Yonema "Bill" Tomiyasu, shown here in 1923 with his children, grew a variety of fruits and vegetables. At its peak in the early 1930s, the farm supplied tons of produce to Six Companies, Inc., to feed workers at the Boulder Dam construction site. Tomiyasu came from a farming family near Nagasaki, Japan, and had immigrated to the United States in 1898 when he was just sixteen. Although he initially started out by picking fruit in San Jose, the ambitious immigrant soon took on gardening and nursery jobs. In 1910, he was working as a

LEFT: Nearby Tomiyasu Lane has been home to the rich and famous over the years, including Clark Gable, Carole Lombard, Gladys Knight, Mike Tyson, Thomas "the Hitman" Hearns, and Wayne Newton.

cook in an Elks Lodge in San Bernardino when one of the members told him about the agricultural promise offered by Las Vegas. Unlike California, which frowned upon Japanese property ownership, there were no such problems in Nevada. In 1914, Tomiyasu purchased forty acres in Las Vegas, and moved there permanently in 1916. An arranged "picture marriage" followed in 1917, along with four children, all of whom helped their father in the backbreaking work of planting and harvesting a large range of crops. During World War II, Tomiyasu, who largely avoided the backlash that affected most Japanese Americans in the West at this time, supplied produce and poultry for the mess hall at the Army Air Corps Gunnery School in Las Vegas.

ABOVE: In the 1960s, the Tomiyasu family lost their farm in a controversial foreclosure that made Las Vegas headlines. The ranch house was torn down and the valuable property was subdivided and sold. Gated, multimillion-dollar homes now cover the area where fields of produce once flourished. Tomiyasu Lane (above left), located just west of Pecos and Warm Springs, is one of the few reminders of the Tomiyasu legacy in this area. The family's botanical legacy can be found throughout southern Nevada in the various types of flora that the Tomiyasus helped to cultivate in Las Vegas. Bill Y. Tomiyasu Elementary School on South Annie Oakley Drive was also named as a tribute and is probably one of the only schools in Clark County to feature a Japanese-style garden for the children.

c.1930

LAS VEGAS HIGH SCHOOL
Alma mater of Air Force hero Lieutenant William Harrell Nellis

ABOVE: Built in 1930 to replace the old mission-style structure on Fifth Street, the Las Vegas High School was designed by the Reno firm of George A. Ferris & Son in a variation of Art Deco style described as "Aztec Moderne." At the time, the school's location at Seventh and Bridger was criticized for being too remote, but fears that the school would never attract enough students were eased when it filled to capacity just two years after opening. Over the years, the school has graduated students who have gone on to become some of Las Vegas's most prominent citizens. These include Lieutenant William H. Nellis, the heroic World War II fighter pilot for whom Nellis Air Force Base was named in 1950. Other alumni include U.S. federal judge Lloyd D. George, former Nevada governor Richard Bryan, and the Rhythmettes. In 1949, Evelyn Stuckey, the school's physical education teacher, formed the Rhythmettes, a group of girls who performed dance and drill routines. Members of the group were required to have a high grade-point average.

ABOVE: One of the success stories of Las Vegas historic preservation, the Las Vegas High School building was entered on the National Register of Historic Places in September 1986. In 1993, a new Las Vegas High School campus was constructed near the foothills of Frenchman's Mountain at the east end of Sahara Avenue, and the original building on Seventh Street became the Las Vegas Academy of International Studies, Performing and Visual Arts. In addition to stewarding the advancement of youth in the arts, the institution serves the community through live performances featuring tomorrow's superstars in this magnificent historic building. The school's theater put on its first production, *Anatomy of Gray* by Jim Leonard Jr., in 1995. The first decade of the twenty-first century has seen some significant cosmetic changes occur in the historic

building's appearance. In 2007, controversy erupted when the campus decided to erect a new electronic sign that the Las Vegas Historical Preservation Commission felt would block views of the school and detract from the historic look of the building. After some modification, however, the sign was approved and now provides an ever-changing display of the school's extensive activities. Even greater change was in store for the historic structure when an extensive paint job gave the building a whole new look. Since its inception, the Las Vegas Academy has continued one Las Vegas High School tradition: producing famous graduates. Some notable graduates of the performing arts program in recent years have been Matthew Gray Gubler of *Criminal Minds* fame and Julianne Hough, best known as a professional dancer on *Dancing with the Stars*.

1964

UNIVERSITY OF NEVADA, LAS VEGAS

From "Tumbleweed Tech" to premier urban university

ABOVE: In the early 1950s, Clark County's dramatic population growth prompted Las Vegas community leaders to appeal to the University of Nevada regents in Reno for the establishment of an extension campus in Las Vegas. In 1957, Nevada Southern University was established on sixty acres in Paradise Valley, just two miles east of the Strip. An aerial view looking west around 1960 shows Maude Frazier Hall (left), Archie C. Grant Hall (right), and the gymnasium in the background. In 1964, Nevada Southern University held its first commencement; its twenty-nine graduates were designated the "Centennial Class" for the hundreth anniversary of Nevada's statehood.

ABOVE: Sparse surroundings led some to nickname Nevada Southern University "Tumbleweed Tech" in its early years, but in 1969, the campus was officially designated the University of Nevada, Las Vegas (UNLV). Although UNLV initially had a strong athletic focus, recent years have seen it develop into a research-oriented university. Dramatic growth over the years has enlarged the campus significantly, as can be seen in this modern aerial view. The first decade of the twenty-first century saw the construction of several new buildings that transformed the campus and the services it provides. These include Lied Library, the Cox Pavilion, the Beam Music Center, the Foundations Building, Greenspun Hall, the Lynn Bennett Early Education Center, the Student Recreation and Wellness Center, the Dayton Complex dormitory, and last but not least, the new student union. In 2007, the university celebrated its fiftieth anniversary, and in 2009, it completed a successful capital campaign called "Invent the Future" that raised $500 million in cash and pledges for the university. Today, Archie C. Grant Hall is still conspicuous at an angle to what is now South Maryland Parkway.

1931

HOOVER DAM
One of the greatest engineering feats of modern America

1934

ABOVE: The immense size of the Hoover Dam meant that its construction could not be formed through a single continuous concrete pour, as it would take 125 years to cool. The solution was to pour the concrete into the smaller, individual column forms through which first cool river water and then ice-cold water was piped in to cure the concrete.

OPPOSITE/LEFT: The solution to years of destructive flooding along the Colorado River, the construction of Boulder (later Hoover) Dam just thirty miles outside Las Vegas was a boon to the local economy. This view shows a pristine Black Canyon looking upstream in 1931, just before construction on the dam began. Thousands of dam workers came to Las Vegas to spend their paychecks, and many more tourists came to see the construction site and visit the city that billed itself as the "Gateway to Boulder Dam." As no single builder could manage the construction of such an immense project, six large contracting firms banded together to form the Six Companies and were able to win the complex dam contract with a bid of $48,890,955 ($5 million under the next bidder). The need to house the thousands of dam workers and their families resulted in the construction of Boulder City on the outskirts of the dam's construction site. City manager Sims Ely ruled with an iron fist, determined to keep the city free from the temptations offered by nearby Las Vegas.

RIGHT: Completed two years ahead of schedule, Boulder Dam was dedicated on September 30, 1935, by President Franklin D. Roosevelt. In 1947, Congress changed its name to Hoover Dam in honor of the former president. Over seventy-five years later, it remains a wonder of modern engineering, attracting a million visitors annually and generating four billion kilowatt-hours of electricity. Congestion on U.S. Highway 93 as it crossed Hoover Dam led to the construction of the Hoover Dam Bypass bridge (left) beginning in January 2005, nearly seventy years after the completion of the dam itself. Located just 1,500 feet downstream of Hoover Dam, the 2,000-foot-long bridge was an engineering marvel that rivaled the dam itself.